C000151510

Your
Horoscope
2023

....

Gemini

22 May – 21 June

igloobooks

igloobooks

Published in 2022
First published in the UK by Igloo Books Ltd
An imprint of Igloo Books Ltd
Cottage Farm, NN6 0BJ, UK
Owned by Bonnier Books
Sveavägen 56, Stockholm, Sweden
www.igloobooks.com

Copyright © 2022 Igloo Books Ltd

All rights reserved. No part of this publication may be
reproduced or transmitted in any form or by any means,
electronic, or mechanical, including photocopying, recording,
or by any information storage and retrieval system,
without permission in writing from the publisher.

0722 001
2 4 6 8 10 9 7 5 3 1
ISBN 978-1-80108-401-7

Written by Sally Kirkman
Additional content by Belinda Campbell and Denise Evans

Cover designed by Richard Sykes
Interiors designed by Chris Stanley
Edited by Luke Robertson

Printed and manufactured in China

CONTENTS
....

INTRODUCTION
. . . .

This 15-month guide has been designed and written to give a concise and accessible insight into both the nature of your star sign and the year ahead. Divided into two main sections, the first part of this guide will give you an overview of your character in order to help you understand how you think, perceive the world and interact with others and – perhaps just as importantly – why. You'll soon see that your zodiac sign is not just affected by a few stars in the sky, but by planets, elements and a whole host of other factors, too.

The second part of this guide is made up of daily forecasts. Use these to increase your awareness of what might appear on your horizon so that you're better equipped to deal with the days ahead. While this should never be used to dictate your life, it can be useful to see how your energies might be affected or influenced, which in turn can help you prepare for what life might throw your way.

By the end of these 15 months, these two sections should have given you a deeper understanding and awareness of yourself and, in turn, the world around you. There are never any certainties in life, but with an open mind you will find guidance for what might be, and learn to take more control of your own destiny.

THE CHARACTER OF THE TWINS

. . . .

Expect a triple dose of conversation, charisma and intellect from Geminians. Not usually satisfied with focusing on one thing at a time, these artful communicators will likely be Tweeting celebrities, texting colleagues and Snapchatting friends simultaneously without even breaking a sweat. Fortunately, they often have twice as much energy as everyone else, so won't usually have an issue keeping up with their active social lives. Lively and affable, Geminians are friends, or at least good acquaintances, with everyone around them. Frequently found fluttering from friend to friend, these social butterflies touch the lives of many.

Geminians crave constant mental stimulation, which is perhaps why they are well known for being intelligent. They are expert conversationalists and are formidable opponents in a debate. Yet, as much as Geminians are happy to lead or even dominate a conversation, they are also just as eager to listen. They have an eternal curiosity, and are keen to learn all the facts about a story that has captured their interest, be it serious news or the latest celebrity break-up. This love for knowledge leads Geminians to learn many secrets, but their athletic approach to conversing often results in them running around and sharing what they've discovered with everyone else. They would be wise to keep gossip to a minimum and instead apply their knack for narrative to writing, like fellow Geminians Arthur Conan Doyle and Salman Rushdie.

THE TWINS

Double the trouble or twice the fun? The Twins that represent
Gemini are an indication of many opposing traits. Castor
and Pollux were twin half-brothers from Greek mythology
who have commonly been portrayed as the Gemini symbol.
In some stories, Castor is thought to be mortal, while Pollux
is immortal. When Castor dies, he is sent to the Underworld
ruled by Hades, leaving Pollux in Olympus with the Gods. The
light and dark of this tale is a perfect example of the two sides
that many Geminians are commonly thought to display. Their
moods are changeable, which may sometimes make them
appear deceitful or two-faced, while their mutability makes
them strong advocates of change. Whether it's altering their
hair colour or even their postcode, these fluid beings are often
unrecognisable from one day to the next. However, Geminians
are fascinating characters to try and get to know.

MERCURY

Orbiting the Sun faster than any other planet in the Solar System, travel and speed are two associations that Geminians surely inherit from their ruling planet Mercury. Named after the Roman god of communication, trickery and travel, winged Mercury is a perfect embodiment of air sign Gemini. The speed at which we travel and communicate is ever increasing, much to the joy of quick-thinking Geminians. Feeling the influence of Mercury, they favour instantly gratifying forms of interaction. However, texting, Tweeting and talking rapidly means that Geminians don't always think before they speak or press send. 'Mercury in retrograde' is a phrase that is often met with fearful faces, but what does it mean? Three times a year, Mercury begins to move backwards in Earth's sky in relation to the other planets, and this is blamed for many communication, media, technology and travel failures or mix-ups. It's a good idea to focus on clarity during these times; precision can help to avoid misunderstandings.

ELEMENTS, MODES AND POLARITIES

Each sign is made up of a unique combination of three defining groups: elements, modes and polarities. Each of these defining parts can manifest themselves in good and bad ways, and none should be seen as a positive or a negative – including the polarities! Just like a jigsaw puzzle, piecing these groups together can help illuminate why each sign has certain characteristics and help us find a balance.

ELEMENTS

Fire: Dynamic and adventurous, signs with fire in them are often extroverted. Others are naturally drawn to them because of the positive light they give off, as well as their high levels of energy and confidence.

Earth: Signs with the earth element are steady and driven. They make for solid friends, parents and partners due to their grounded influence and nurturing nature.

Air: The invisible element that influences each of the other elements significantly, air signs provide much-needed perspective to those around them with their fair thinking, verbal skills and key ideas.

Water: Warm in the shallows but sometimes as freezing as ice, the emotional depth and empathy of this mysterious element is essential to the growth of everything around it.

MODES

Cardinal: Pioneers of the calendar, cardinal signs jump-start each season and are the energetic go-getters.

Fixed: Marking the middle of the calendar, fixed signs firmly denote and value both steadiness and reliability.

Mutable: As the seasons end, the mutable signs adapt and gladly give themselves over to the promise of change.

POLARITIES

Positive: Typically extroverted, positive signs take physical action and embrace external stimulus in their life.

Negative: Usually introverted, negative signs value emotional development and experiencing life from the inside out.

GEMINI IN BRIEF

The table below shows the key attributes of Geminians.
Use it for quick reference and to understand more about
this fascinating sign.

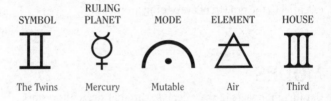

SYMBOL	RULING PLANET	MODE	ELEMENT	HOUSE
The Twins	Mercury	Mutable	Air	Third

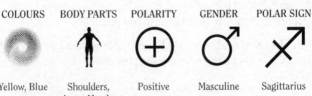

COLOURS	BODY PARTS	POLARITY	GENDER	POLAR SIGN
Yellow, Blue	Shoulders, Arms, Hands, Nervous System	Positive	Masculine	Sagittarius

ROMANTIC RELATIONSHIPS

Like their element of air, Geminians have a lightness to them that lifts others up. However, anyone who falls for these flyaway characters will need to work hard to keep their interests piqued. Geminians can reach dizzying heights of ecstasy in love but soon lose their curiosity, leaving partners plummeting back to Earth painfully. They are likely to have several potential love interests simultaneously, and will be quick to abandon conversations if they get bored. Speed dating could make for an interesting night out for this fast-paced chatterbox!

With a love of change and speed, Geminians often walk away from relationships too quickly. To hold onto a relationship, they will need to slow down and take a moment to honestly discuss whatever issues need to be addressed. Nothing is perfect, and the most worthwhile endeavours are usually those that take time and effort – something that Geminians would do well to consider in their love lives. While they are expert communicators, taking the time to pause and reflect on problems in a relationship will probably not come easily, and will be something they need to work hard at.

Not ones to take themselves too seriously, Geminians will appreciate energetic lovers that they can have fun with. Thanks to their mutability, they can be very easy-going in relationships and are unlikely to fight for control. They usually value partners who are similarly relaxed, but also could be attracted to more forthright types who take the lead and encourage them to explore new heights. Keep curious Geminians intrigued and their love will be invigorating.

ARIES: COMPATIBILITY 4/5

Though very different in their approaches to relationships, these two positive signs can bring out the very best in one another. Communication is key for any relationship, and the Geminian's talkative nature can help the Arian to vocalise dreams and ideas. These two can form an intellectual bond that lays a strong foundation for love. The Twins and Ram are both guilty of starting projects and not finishing them, which can extend to their relationship with each other. However, their similarities and positive natures are likely to still see them part as friends if the romance is extinguished.

TAURUS: COMPATIBILITY 2/5

Three may prove to be a crowd where Gemini and Taurus are concerned. The duality of a Geminian, characterised in the Twin symbol, can make a Taurean feel uneasy about starting a romantic relationship. The earth sign of Taurus mixed with airy Gemini may not be an easy partnership, but if the Taurean can budge on set ideas, love could blossom. The Geminian's communication skills help when understanding the Taurean's needs, providing the love and security that is craved, while Taurus can help Gemini learn to adopt a calmer pace. Communication, trust and flexibility should be this couple's mantra if they are to go the distance.

GEMINI: COMPATIBILITY 4/5

A Geminian couple is likely to be a roaring hit at social gatherings. This pair will share stimulating conversations until the early hours of the morning, and probably still be energised enough to make a brunch date. Life might feel like a constant party when two Geminians unite, but they may struggle to connect on a deeper emotional level. These smart thinkers match each other in many ways, so this relationship will be full of shared thoughts and exciting adventures.

CANCER: COMPATIBILITY 2/5

This air and water pairing can feel too far apart personality-wise to make a good match, but in some cases their differences may actually prove to be a strength. The Geminian is led by the mind and the Cancerian by emotion, and these contrasting perspectives can lead to misunderstandings and arguments if the line of communication isn't clear. The Geminian can help the Cancerian communicate thoughts and feelings aloud rather than keeping them bottled up, while the Cancerian can provide lessons on the value of sensitivity. With so much to learn from one another, understanding and acceptance is vital to the success of this partnership.

LEO: COMPATIBILITY 4/5

The Leonian's inner youth might be just what the energetic sign of Gemini asked for. This love can be like a fantasy story, full of love and adventure. The high-energy Leonian was born to lead, while the mutable Geminian is happy to take this Lion's hand and fly speedily off into a fantasy world. The Leonian will encourage the Geminian to take an active part in the important choices in their lives. Both positive signs, their extrovert energies and curious natures will see this air and fire match embark on endless adventures.

VIRGO: COMPATIBILITY 1/5

While a Virgoan may be attracted to a Geminian's charm and wit, they could soon feel irritated by the recurring flights of fancy. The steady Virgoan might feel too reserved for the Geminian, while the fast-paced Geminian can be too much for the Virgoan. Both ruled by Mercury and strong believers in communication, these otherwise contrasting characters may end up feeling as if they are speaking two completely different languages. However, these signs combined are nothing if not unpredictable, and their mutual love of change and talent for adaptability may well be what makes this relationship last.

LIBRA: COMPATIBILITY 3/5

With Libra ruled by the planet of love, Venus, and Gemini by the planet of communication, Mercury, this partnership will be founded on a strong base of affection and understanding. The debate-loving Geminian and peace-seeking Libran will likely have their conflicts, but if love troubles do arise, these two are likely to have the verbal skills and creative thinking needed to work out their issues. While both often have trouble making up their minds, the Libran's cardinal instinct usually sets in to help make the course of action clear, much to the delight of the mutable Geminian.

SCORPIO: COMPATIBILITY 3/5

Passionate debates are definitely on the agenda when Scorpio and Gemini come together. Scorpio's water element will bring emotional depth to the relationship, while the air influence from the Geminian will help breathe a fresh perspective into things. The Geminian can at times be flirtatious, flighty or unreliable, and this can be tricky for Scorpio to deal with. As a fixed sign who values steadiness, too much unpredictability can trigger Scorpio's feelings of insecurity. However, with both partners ready to speak their minds, this relationship has the potential to be full of spice and interest.

. . . .

SAGITTARIUS: COMPATIBILITY 5/5

'I love you just the way you are' could be the vows of a strongly independent Sagittarian and Geminian. Despite both being mutable and willing to adapt, there is unlikely to be anything about this match that either partner will want to change about the other. As opposite signs on the zodiac calendar, the love between the Sagittarian and Geminian is almost always going to be unique. For the easily bored Geminian, the adventurous Sagittarian is a perfect fit, ensuring that this couple has endless days of love and fun ahead.

CAPRICORN: COMPATIBILITY 1/5

This earth and air coupling may be an unlikely match, but an awareness of their differences could help create a strong bond. The Capricornian appreciates tangible things like a good career and a beautiful home, while the Geminian loves exciting ideas and the invisible workings of the mind. Even though Gemini's mutable element fits well with the Capricorn's cardinal aspect, what drives the Capricornian may be at odds with what drives the Geminian. This polar-opposite couple – the Capricornian negative and the Geminian positive – may struggle to find common ground, but with a little patience, they could learn a lot from each other.

AQUARIUS: COMPATIBILITY 4/5

An individualist Aquarian and dual-personality Geminian often make for a compatible trio. Born in the eleventh house, which signifies community and friendship, the Aquarian thrives in groups and will be a fantastic partner to the social butterfly Geminian. Mutable in nature, the Geminian is happy to follow the Aquarian's fixed lead, which will likely bring a steadiness to the relationship. Both share the element of air and are positive, so are likely to have a lot in common. With the Geminian's love of change and the Aquarian's need for progress, these two could create a bright and revolutionary future together.

PISCES: COMPATIBILITY 3/5

As fluid as water and as free flowing as air, a Piscean and Geminian can experience an extremely flexible and forgiving relationship if they fall for one another. Both mutable, this couple is highly compatible and will not fight for leadership, and instead prefer to rule side by side. While these two may not always understand each other perfectly, their open-minded attitudes will help resolve any disagreements. While the Geminian is led by the tricky influence of Mercury, the Piscean's water influence means that they are both often ruled by their emotions. A meeting of heads and hearts will be key.

FAMILY AND FRIENDS

. . . .

'You think you know someone, and then you find out they're a Gemini'. That's the sentiment friends and family of Geminians may express. To truly know Geminians is to be able to identify their light and dark sides, their love of gossip and their passion for politics. Geminians should try to get to know both sides of themselves just as much as their friends and family should. Their duality means they are extremely good at acting as go-betweens to friends and families; able to see two sides to every story, Geminians can act as a bridge of communication between two contrasting sides, making them excellent peacemakers. Although they may sometimes instigate debates that turn into arguments, their knack for seeing multiple perspectives makes them a voice of reason that shouldn't be ignored.

Whether it's about global politics, last night's game or the food on their plate, Geminians will have an opinion about everything and will debate it to the death. Not necessarily in it to win it, they have endless curiosity and enjoy being tested and presented with new ways of thinking, as this satisfies their love of learning. Rather than shy away from friends or family who challenge their intellect, Geminians will usually try harder to hold on to stimulating relationships, so be sure to bring the most exciting conversation to one of their infamous dinner parties. However, if they aren't to be entertained, they will move on swiftly, abandoning a dull conversation and searching for something of more interest elsewhere. Geminians don't attempt to conceal their dwindling interest, so anyone wishing to hold their attention should watch closely and be ready to change the subject!

FAMILY AND FRIENDS

Being related to Geminians, who carry the element of air, can sometimes feel like being caught up in a gale-force wind. Those closest will see them at their stormiest and strongest. Perhaps the quote often attributed to Geminian Marilyn Monroe best sums it up: "If you can't handle me at my worst, then you sure as hell don't deserve me at my best". Geminians talk non-stop and with endless energy, but if friends and family aren't left exhausted, they will no doubt feel enlivened. Their need for constant change, even in relationships, mean that the dynamics between family and friends constantly evolve and change. Having the mental energy to keep up with Geminians will be a task and a half, but can have exciting rewards. The young energy of Leonians makes them perfect playmates, while fellow Geminians are sure to be a source of fun.

MONEY AND CAREERS

· · · · · · · · · · · · · · · · · ·

Being a particular star sign will not dictate certain types of career, but it can help to identify potential areas to thrive in. To succeed in the workplace, it is important to understand your strengths and weaknesses, which will help in choosing and achieving career and financial goals.

The planet Mercury is thought to be able to change the way that people think, just like the influential Geminians who are ruled by it. These charismatic characters have a silver tongue and are more than capable of imprinting their intellect and ideas on those they encounter. They will likely have an aptitude for sales, but sometimes what they sell best is themselves. Kings, queens, prime ministers and presidents, Geminians have been ruling the world for decades. Strategy, intellect, communication and the desire and ability to create change are defining features of both Geminians and successful leaders. They have a great ability to multitask, so are usually best suited to a career that challenges them intellectually; a career in politics could therefore be worth pursuing.

The youth associated with Mercury gives Geminians an eternal vitality, but could also mean that they are prone to making blunders. Fortunately, they love learning, so will usually grow from their mistakes. A teaching environment could be well suited to Geminians, as their ability to communicate and their influential way of thinking should make them favourites amongst their pupils. The annual changeover of students would also be a bonus for mutable Geminians, as long as the lessons themselves aren't too repetitive. They can become bored easily, so will not remain happy in a job that stays the same or prevents them from evolving in some way. Their love of words and narrative means that writing could be where their talents are best suited, as is the case with Geminian Salman Rushdie.

As with family, colleagues cannot be chosen. It can therefore be advantageous to use star signs to learn about their key characteristics and discover the best ways of working together. Sharing the element of air, Librans and Aquarians will connect with Geminians on a thoughtful level and can make inspiring and influential colleagues. Geminian Paul McCartney and Libran John Lennon are a great example of the dizzying heights that these two deep thinking star signs can help each other reach. Steady Taureans are likely to lock horns with flighty Geminians over their advocacy for change in a work environment, and sometimes Geminians may be reluctant to engage with Taureans' more methodical approach. Both methods have their time to shine. An extra dollop of patience and understanding should be served up if they find themselves on the same team.

HEALTH AND WELLBEING

Moved by their air element, Geminians are full of ideas and insights that will usually be heard loud and clear thanks to the influence of Mercury, the planet signifying communication. Conversely, if Geminians feel like their voices aren't being listened to, their health and wellbeing may soon deteriorate. While mutable Geminians are usually happy to go along with the plans of others, it's vital that they make their imprint in some way if they are to be content and true to themselves.

As much as Geminians advocate diversity in their lives and surroundings, they should also celebrate the complicated diversity within themselves. They are sometimes accused of being dishonest, but their duality is an important part of their uniqueness that they should learn to embrace. Capable of being the life and soul of a party, Geminians are also prone to feeling overwhelmed, and may sometimes need to find some space for themselves. Their social sides should be exercised just as much as their quieter, more thoughtful aspects to help maintain a healthy emotional balance. Geminians should try to surround themselves with friends and family that allow them to show off their charming side and that challenge their intellect, but don't require them to be 'switched on' at all times. Ultimately, they should strive to find the right balance by making room to enjoy each aspect of their changeable personality.

Geminians can be eager to move on quickly from things, including their feelings. They like to remain light-hearted and can be guilty of only skimming the surface of things. Delving deeply into their emotions might initially feel suffocating to Geminians, but the practise of looking at their underlying emotions and desires can lead them away from living a purely shallow existence and bring a deeper resonance to their lives. By pausing and focusing more time and energy into themselves and their relationships, Geminians can reap the rewards that they don't usually receive from their more impatient behaviour.

The part of the human body most associated with Gemini is the nervous system. It ensures the body acts in the way that the brain tells it to, which is perhaps why communication is so closely connected to this sign. If they choose to ignore the signals from their bodies telling them to slow down, Geminians can push themselves mentally and physically to the point of exhaustion. While it is not in their nature to slow down, even energetic Geminians will tire eventually. They may be able to pre-empt a burnout by taking the time to switch off from the constant chatter of their outside life and focusing on their internal health. Regular screen breaks and time away from technology will give their overactive minds a much-needed rest. A peaceful retreat somewhere with terrible phone reception and no internet signal may be just what the doctor ordered.

Gemini

. . . .

DAILY FORECASTS
for 2022

OCTOBER

. . . .

Saturday 1st

Reach out for something new and expansive today. Broaden your mind but remember your limits. It's possible that you might push too far and cross a boundary, causing some upset this evening. You may also be required by family and friends, even if you're reluctant to tear yourself away from a partner.

Sunday 2nd

Mercury turns direct, so you may realise that you have been looking at something the wrong way. Your inner compass can guide you now, but you will need to do the groundwork yourself. Go over recent events and see what still holds value and attracts you.

Monday 3rd

Ease yourself into the week by taking small steps in your tasks. It would be helpful to bring out your inner genius to look for better ways to approach problems. A breakthrough may happen if you move away from traditional ways of working.

Tuesday 4th

Your outgoing mood and busy mind mean that connecting and networking with others is likely to be important to you. You have the advantage today as good energy breathes fresh air into old relating patterns. You may learn something that attracts you to do more for the wider world and your partnerships.

Wednesday 5th

Feeling stuck is often an invitation to pause and reflect. You might be learning a lot right now, but this will need practical application too. A teacher or respected friend may show you how to do something from which you can learn more about self-discipline and when to act.

Thursday 6th

Impress people with your flexibility and show off your ability to adapt well to new things. Going with the flow should come easily today, so you should feel light and optimistic. Your creative side could merge with your work duties today.

Friday 7th

If there's a project that needs doing before the weekend, spend your energy on that. This may involve a family issue, a thorough clean-up or discarding something that is now obsolete. Make space and lighten your duties to allow new opportunities to come in and inspire you to grow.

Saturday 8th

You might be feeling tired and worry that you're being lazy. Take a day off to play around with your inner compass. Be prepared to listen to other people's opinions, even if they aren't helpful or informed. A social activity could be fun and might be the push you need to drag you out of a slump.

Sunday 9th

Pluto turns direct and continues through your intimacy sector, asking you to get deep and meaningful with the people you value. A full moon might show the completion of a project within your social groups, but may also expose those who aren't pulling their weight. Share duties in a combined cause.

Monday 10th

The day begins with great energy that should keep you motivated and on task. However, you may need to use practical rather than mental skills this afternoon, especially if a new task requires a plan that feels slow to you. Keep it attainable and don't rush into things.

Tuesday 11th

Mercury returns to your creative and romantic zone, so you may feel playful and childlike. Unfiltered communication might surface in a relationship now. This energy will also be good for painting, poetry and music. If you express yourself freely, your work and home duties will feel balanced and refreshed.

Wednesday 12th

You might be moody today, especially if things aren't going your way. It's possible that restless energy and the inability to use it makes you throw a tantrum or sulk. An evening alone will help you to withdraw from tension and realign with your true north. You may need to restart a project.

Thursday 13th

The moon in your sign will make you feel more like yourself, so you should be feeling more inquisitive today. Your mental activity is high, so you should be overflowing with creative ideas that you would like to get off the ground soon. This is also a good day for laughing until your belly hurts.

Friday 14th

A day of air energy will bring you more harmony, fun, love and compassion. Your heart may be wide open and you might be willing to go the extra mile for someone special. Perhaps you can plan a trip together for some time in the future or research cultures that interest you.

Saturday 15th

You may be highly motivated, especially if you're ready for a packed weekend. However, you may also choose to stay at home and enjoy your own environment. Hosting a party or event for friends might be a good idea if you can organise it with no hiccups or big egos clashing.

Sunday 16th

A need for security may conflict with your need to connect today. Your indecision could drain your mental resources and cause you to do nothing. Think about your daily routines and private life. How much do you want to share? Perhaps you need to open up a little.

Monday 17th

It's likely that you have scratched an old wound and now have a sore spot. You may feel that you're doing more for others and not enough for yourself. If you think you're off track or being dragged out of your comfort zone, reassess where your time goes.

Tuesday 18th

You might be more outspoken and attempt to voice a few grievances today. Look at what you learn about yourself by doing this. If friends and social groups aren't giving you the kick that you need right now, you may feel that you would be better valued elsewhere.

Wednesday 19th

Spending time with a lover or creative project can help to balance some emotions that you're uncomfortable with. You might be extra assertive today, and your self-expression could be shocking to some. If you wish to have your boundaries respected, then you must do the same for others. Don't dig deeper holes for yourself by speaking without compassion.

Thursday 20th

Your relationships might be tested now. You may not like someone probing too deeply, but try to communicate positively and with strength. A partner may be more understanding than you expect and prefer to see you happy and balanced than stressed about where a relationship may be going.

Friday 21st

Use today to think about how much you are willing to share in a relationship. Privacy may be important, especially in keeping your heart guarded against disappointment. Try an unconditional approach to love and let your partner share a few things with you in return.

Saturday 22nd

More discussions may be needed in order to move on with a relationship. Family members may offer well-intentioned advice, but this could also conflict with your wish to be aligned with your truth. Try to explain that if something doesn't feel right to you, there's no point spending energy on it.

Sunday 23rd

Saturn turns direct and opens up an area where you may have felt blocked. Consider settling something in your love life or accepting things the way they are. The emphasis may now be on intense exchanges or serving each other's needs, and this could deepen your connection with those closest to you.

Monday 24th

A weight will be lifted from your mind if a decision is taken out of your hands today . This may be the best resolution, especially if you're now able to have emotional discussions and lay some ground rules for moving on.

Tuesday 25th

A new moon and solar eclipse open a window to some wildcard energy. This can be an intensely loving time, and things may also be sexy and seductive. Stay open-minded and see where things go over the next two weeks. Make time in your schedule for intimacy and deep discussions.

Wednesday 26th

Thinking back to past times may not be the best idea today, especially if doing so opens a wound you thought had healed. You may be feeling vulnerable now, especially if you're not used to this level of intensity in a relationship. Use your communication skills to try to get to the bottom of these feelings before they eat you up.

Thursday 27th

Emotions continue to flow, so you may be sharing your dreams and visions with someone special. Discussions often motivate you to be your best self, especially those in your area of expertise. You might be dating this afternoon, or perhaps you're stepping outside your comfort zone with a partner.

Friday 28th

Jupiter is in retrograde and enters your career zone as if to tell you that there's something you need to complete. This may come as an inconvenience, but could ultimately bring you some bonuses. An open heart allows you to connect with groups who do great things for the wider world.

Saturday 29th

You may be tired today after the recent high levels of activity. However, you may need to rush to make a deal or set something in stone with a partner. Slow down and know that there are many steps to take before making a commitment. Time for deep introspection is coming.

Sunday 30th

Mars turns retrograde in your star sign, and this should prompt you to take stock of what you have learned and slow your pace for a few months. If you're highly motivated, you may find this time difficult or frustrating. Don't do anything impulsive simply for the sake of it.

Monday 31st

A measure of self-control might help you to deal with something that has been problematic in the workplace. You may have to be tough on someone or pull back from your many projects. Look at things from many different perspectives, use empathy and find a workable solution for all involved.

NOVEMBER
· · · · · · · · · · · · · · · · · ·

Tuesday 1st

This is likely to be a challenging day, so you might not get much done. It could be an emotional rollercoaster, causing your busy mind to turn this way and that. Sharing, caring and privacy are important themes, while old wounds are reopened.

Wednesday 2nd

You may experience a lack of energy and motivation today, especially if lines of enquiry seem to lead nowhere. It will take some dedication on your part to stick to one thing and follow it through. By evening, you may be much more flexible or wish to spend time alone on self-care and nostalgic thoughts.

Thursday 3rd

Another emotional day awaits, but it is still possible to be productive. Use your powers of investigation to discover avenues you would like to explore more. You might learn some deep and mysterious lessons which teach you more about yourself, especially if you have been reluctant to share your inner world with someone special.

Friday 4th

Your inner compass directs you to dig up old behaviours and get rid of them once and for all. This won't be a quick fix, but if you can dedicate yourself to some study or guidance, you will embrace your psyche and pull out the gold hidden within.

Saturday 5th

New groups may be a big help now, and you should find that collective energy that suits where you are on your path. It could be a karmic time, especially if you have a visitor from the past. This could be an emotional trigger for you, but it might also be an opportunity to learn.

Sunday 6th

It's a good time to make plans to travel in a different way. Listen to your inner voice and put your energy and motivation into doing your inner work. Try not to be distracted by voices of self-doubt. The deeper you go with this, the better.

Monday 7th

You might struggle today, especially if you're keen to be left alone to investigate your inner workings. Duties and obligations may distract you, so consider making and sticking to a schedule that encompasses everything you'd like to do. Don't be seduced by projects that are too big for you.

Tuesday 8th

A full moon and a lunar eclipse light up the parts of you that require the most healing. Use your Gemini skills to research these issues before diving in, and take care that this doesn't lead to stress or other health problems. You might need the help of a trusted guide.

Wednesday 9th

An inclination to speak without thinking may cause some tension now. Somebody, maybe you, might speak out or expose an old hurt that you thought you had dealt with. Take time to process this before making any assumptions that prevent you from carrying on with your studies.

Thursday 10th

You might be pretty stubborn today and refuse to move on until others have acknowledged your feelings. You may retract a favour or clash with authority. However, there is also the right kind of energy to realign with your true north. Consider whether you need to change your perspective.

Friday 11th

Blocks and restrictions may impede your progress today. The trick is to not take these issues personally. This is a good time to pause, reflect and review your progress so far. A rest stop on your journey may show you alternate routes or help you to feel proud of your efforts to date. Be gentle with yourself now.

Saturday 12th

If you feel over-sensitive today, take a weekend off and spend time alone. This is a good time to snuggle down with a blanket and a favourite movie or book. Escape into fantasy land for a while. The world will still be there waiting for you when you're ready to reconnect.

Sunday 13th

Stay in your safety zone and look around at the world. Do material things give you security? If you feel protected and nourished by your environment, don't change a thing. If items are taking up space that could be better used, remove them. Make your space one to be proud of.

Monday 14th

You may already be noticing the effect that your inner investigations are having. Getting to the bottom of your conditioned behaviours can help you to act differently when similar triggers come along. You may feel ready to put this to the test, but be mindful when expressing yourself.

Tuesday 15th

Check in with your health and ensure that you haven't dismissed anything that needs addressing, including your mental health. Are you taking care of your own needs? Make time for a treat or a detox today.

Wednesday 16th

Venus enters your relationship zone, followed by your ruler Mercury. This heralds a time when you can express your desires without feeling ashamed. Ask for what you want, as you have more chance of getting it now. Think big and be bold enough to share with a partner.

Thursday 17th

If you are required to go through the details of a family event, you may find that you feel resentful of this, especially if you're caught between partner time and family obligations. Do your best to give everyone the benefit of your methodical and quick mind, but don't let others take advantage of your helpfulness.

Friday 18th

Tremors in your psyche could indicate that you are reacting to situations in a negative way. If you wish to heal and grow, this may need to be changed. You might feel resentful about a person you perceive to be holding you back from your dreams or other activities. Take stock. Is that perception fair?

Saturday 19th

Today you may feel like throwing everything out and starting all over again, but this is not be the best idea. Instead, see this as a test of patience. A partner or close friend may help you to find a reasonable workaround. Be open-minded and ask for what you want. A good listener may be enough.

Sunday 20th

There is more air energy for you to access today. If you feel comfortable, you should be able to get clarity and process things for yourself. There may have been insurmountable limits in your way, but you should now see why they were there.

Monday 21st

Apply more effort to health matters today. An issue may have come to light recently that now needs attention. You may begin to understand the deeper consequences this evening and feel the need to give yourself a good talking to. A healthier diet or a better fitness regime will help you to stop bad habits.

Tuesday 22nd

The Sun moves into your partner zone now. Things could heat up, or you might have more of a yearning to get away and explore. You may see now how old habits and routines have let you down or have accumulated to cause you physical and emotional issues.

Wednesday 23rd

You might be quite stubborn today and resist good advice. Try to see sense and begin to put things in place for an easier transition. Emotions are likely to be up and down as you navigate a new routine and try to see a different perspective.

Thursday 24th

Today comes with many blessings: Jupiter turns direct and eases the pressure at work, while a new moon sets the standard for the next six months in your relationships. You may be experiencing more positive emotions and feel able to discuss your needs with a partner. A corner has been turned.

Friday 25th

If you slip back into negative thinking, know that this is a phase that will pass quickly. Be willing to make a long-term plan for getting to know your body's needs. There's no rush to achieve anything right now, so take it slowly and arm yourself with all of the key information.

Saturday 26th

Stand as an observer of your own life and review what holds value for you. You may notice a shift in your thinking and find that what was once important no longer is. A focus on finances, joint investments and quality goods may be pushed aside in favour of deep investigation into what really makes you tick.

Sunday 27th

Your inner compass is asking if you are still aligned. Your true north may have moved slightly, but it's still there. An inner transformation is taking place, whether you realise it or not. Spiritual movements may be attracting you and could give you some peace and fulfilment.

Monday 28th

If your mental energy seems lacking, try minimising your tasks and breaking them into smaller pieces. You may feel more outgoing today and be willing to learn something new and unusual. However, you should do this gradually to avoid a massive mental overload.

Tuesday 29th

You may encounter a person who can act as a guide or teacher on your path. This will be especially useful if you're ready to hear the answers to many of your questions. Try to be still and absorb what you are taught today. Process this before applying it to your life.

Wednesday 30th

A partner may be the one who shows up as your guiding light now. It's also likely that your shadow is making itself known and that you are learning from your own deepest parts. What comes up now will be here to stay for the long-term, so you must accommodate it.

DECEMBER
. . . .

Thursday 1st
This is a difficult day for reconciling opposing energies. You may be doing your best to bring together lovers or merging the lines of thinking and feeling. Hang on to your inner compass and do what feels right to you. Honour your own values and let everyone else see to their own business.

Friday 2nd
Don't talk yourself out of a good position now, especially if you're offered a great opportunity at work that you'd be foolish to turn down. A supportive partner will help you to expand and grow. Write your thoughts down and review what they mean to you.

Saturday 3rd
Your social groups should be encouraging and there could be a lot of activity in this area today. Friends may look to you for leadership, and you could find that they are strong allies when you have a personal decision to make. There are wheels to be put in motion now.

Sunday 4th
Neptune turns direct, so you should have more clarity about your true north soon. Let the dust settle first, then assess whether your wants and needs have changed. Take time alone and turn inward to find the clarity you seek.

Monday 5th

You may be able to get a better sense of where your future lies today. A deep rumbling in your psyche could feel like a volcano waiting to explode; try to think of it as furniture being rearranged. Some parts of you look better in the light, while other parts prefer to stay in the shade.

Tuesday 6th

If a little voice of indecision whispers, you may falter today. Try to ignore your inner critic, especially if you're more susceptible to self-doubt and low self-esteem. Instead, look at the great work you've done this year and reward yourself. A plan of action may be revealed to you this evening.

Wednesday 7th

Your ruler Mercury has moved into your intimacy zone and is ready to look at how you share with others. You should find that you are now more willing to commit to something which will keep you occupied and stimulated over the festive period.

Thursday 8th

There's a full moon in your sign today, and this is a time to look back at your achievements concerning how you present to the world. You may decide that you have no wish to rush around and instead choose to let the outside world come to you. This could be a moment of recognition.

Friday 9th

New challenges may feel like an attack on your values today, and could cause you to retreat to your safety zone. Your lover might ask more of you than you are willing to give, while work could be asking for something to be completed. Don't get defensive, and instead ask for more time if you need it.

Saturday 10th

Strengthen yourself today by feeding your soul with things you love. A simple day at home surrounded by your treasures will help you to feel recharged and protected. Don't be tempted to follow an impulse to switch things up, as you're likely to regret it later. Get ready to deepen a love interest.

Sunday 11th

Your heart may expand today, while your inner compass points towards more joy and alignment at work. It may be that you have new duties that you are eager to get to grips with. Your safety zone will benefit if you expand your world view and accept that you have much to learn.

Monday 12th

An outgoing mood may have you planning a trip overseas or taking more of an interest in other cultures. Your partner may be keen to travel on this journey with you. Try not to limit yourself or your movements.

Tuesday 13th

When you have an idea in your head, you might often rush to make it real. You may therefore be frustrated by the lack of momentum today. Keep researching or gathering information in preparation. Calm your impulses and let things play out in their own time.

Wednesday 14th

You may find it difficult to be adaptable today, especially if there are too many options to choose from or a lack of clarity makes you stall. Check all the details and confer with family members who may be able to help you slow down.

Thursday 15th

Get grounded today and make your enquiries from a place of solid roots. You may have a lot of information to sort through, so a day of filing and organising could help to calm you. Throw away any intangible ideas.

Friday 16th

If you feel overwhelmed today, keep doing practical things. Exercising or getting out in nature will help. By evening you may have a better sense of balance, and find that thinking and feeling merge easily with creativity and romance.

Saturday 17th

Take a rest stop to allow yourself some quality time. If a relationship is a little suffocating, you may need your own space today. You might be surprised by how a partner reacts to this, especially if they need the same thing. Stay connected and honour each other's choices.

Sunday 18th

Your head and heart could be out of sync, so you may need to escape to fantasy thinking or simply switch off and watch your favourite movies. There may be something you would like to resolve that is out of your control right now. Leave it for another time when you may have more clarity.

Monday 19th

Deeply intense feelings may cause you to return to a loved one now. This might be a past love or a current one with whom you wish to connect on another level. You may notice that old thought patterns are being replaced with new ones and positively changing the way you relate to others.

Tuesday 20th

If an internal shift is happening, you may feel exposed or criticised. However, this is good for you and will help you incorporate the lessons you have learned this year. Your hopes and dreams may take a meaningful turn and have more substance to them now.

Wednesday 21st

The winter solstice arrives, and you might feel like sharing it with someone special. Group celebrations may not be suitable, especially if you prefer to be quiet. This is a window of opportunity to set goals and intentions for the long winter nights ahead. An exploration of the depths of your relationship may appeal to you now.

Thursday 22nd

Think about letting someone else lead you today. Take time to rest and pamper yourself before the festive activities take hold. You can make time for others later, but today should be for you. Let yourself unwind and recharge.

Friday 23rd

Today's new moon is another chance to dedicate more effort towards your intimate relationships. You may see a mountain ahead of you, but if you are determined not to rush, you are more likely to enjoy the journey and reach the summit, where you can gaze at the view with a very special person.

Saturday 24th

You could be on cloud nine today, especially if a lover sweeps you away and woos you with words and gifts. Pleasant surprises await you, and may stir something deep inside. If you're in a particularly good place right now, remember to give gratitude where it's due.

Sunday 25th

Your big heart may try to please everyone at once. There's a general feeling of goodwill on this festive day and for you, it could stretch from close friends to your bigger social groups. There's plenty of fun to be had today with the important people in your life.

Monday 26th

It's possible that you've overdone the good things and don't feel like going anywhere today. You shouldn't feel guilty about this. You could feel irritable if asked to remember your duties and obligations, so try to share the chores with others.

Tuesday 27th

You may feel that simply switching off is in your best interests, so a lazy day could be the ideal thing for you. Binge-watching festive movies and merging easily with loved ones will allow you to unwind while still being part of the team. Everyone can pull together if there's work to do.

Wednesday 28th

Some special time with a lover could reveal what you both desire from the relationship. You may have merged as a couple and now feel able to share dreams and visions. This should make it easier for you to hold on to your inner compass, as you now have someone to keep you steady.

Thursday 29th

Mercury turns retrograde today. This will help you to review shared plans and finances, so long as you remember to be clear in all your communications. There may be big plans within your social groups today that you want to be part of. Get out and enjoy an event with your like-minded friends.

Friday 30th

It might not be a good idea to push against the collective today. You may have fleeting instances of energy, but overall, you're unlikely to have the strength to take on anything that requires assertiveness. Leave these matters for now and enjoy the slower pace of the day. Go along with the general flow of those around you.

Saturday 31st

If you don't want to join the party tonight, you don't have to. The energy suggests that a quiet night at home with a lover, close friend or by yourself could be the best way to end the year. A celebration doesn't have to be big to be meaningful. Have a wonderful close to 2022.

Gemini

....

DAILY FORECASTS
for 2023

JANUARY

. . . .

Sunday 1st

If life is too busy, take a break and slow the pace as the new year begins. It's not the best time to set your resolutions, so consider waiting a few weeks instead. What would help is resolving to turn over a new leaf and make a fresh start.

Monday 2nd

It's a good Bank Holiday for visualisation and daydreaming. Relax into the new year by playing around with different ideas. Try not to let your mood drop today. If you're waiting on a payment or require a financial resolution to an issue, the turning point may come later this month.

Tuesday 3rd

Venus, the planet of relating, lights up your travel and study zone from today, so you may be up for a holiday romance or be reminiscing about a lover who lives abroad. If you're in a relationship, think about planning a romantic break.

Wednesday 4th

There's an educational vibe to love today. Whether you're in a relationship or not, you could find that you're attracted to another person's mind. Being with someone who's easy to talk to can be more fulfilling than sitting next to someone who looks good but has little to say for themselves.

Thursday 5th

Pay close attention to your ideas and instincts. When you choose to do things differently and step out of your normal routine, you access fresh parts of your intuitive brain. Be ready for a moment of genius.

Friday 6th

Today's full moon might coincide with a surprising gift or an offer that benefits you. Alternatively, you might have the chance to help fulfil someone else's dreams. Kindness is always a well-received emotion.

Saturday 7th

Mercury retrograde often shifts the goalposts, so something you thought was final or secure could turn out not to be the best bet. Having said that, this is a positive day to trust your intuition. Notice what appears in your inbox and who pops into your life.

Sunday 8th

This is not be the best time to make a major decision. Instead, try to discuss all your options and listen to other people's ideas. Open the lines of communication and talk about a specific issue to everyone concerned. Be patient and wait for the right moment.

Monday 9th

Venus and Mars, the lovers of the heavens, unite today, and this is particularly exciting if you're revisiting a past love or planning to return to a significant destination with your partner. While you may be slowed down in other ways, your love life should start to open up.

Tuesday 10th

If there's an obstacle in your life that's stopping you from travelling or studying, know that this may shift come the spring. You might want to think about planning a major event in one of these key areas starting in March or April. Put your feet up at home this evening.

Wednesday 11th

If there's an area in life where you've been held back or lacking in energy since late October, Mars's change of direction tomorrow is the planetary equivalent of shifting gears and hitting the accelerator. You should swiftly overcome any limitations as you speed ahead.

Thursday 12th

Mars represents dynamic energy, so notice if you feel more passionate, angry or emotional today. Whatever you've been working on in private, this might be a good time to launch a new initiative and take what you've learned out into the world.

Friday 13th

Put your brain to good use today by coming up with some creative ideas. Manifestation techniques could help, so close your eyes and start wishing. It's a good evening for a first date or a night out with your partner. The one subject you might want to avoid is money.

Saturday 14th

If you're in a new relationship, consider spending time with your partner today. Keep things light when it comes to love and try to avoid any serious or taboo issues. Being around a family member would be a wonderful way to make the most of some feel-good vibes.

Sunday 15th

Travel or study plans could be altered or changed in some way today. This may not necessarily be a bad thing, so be flexible and try to work things out in light of the new options available. If you're looking for a fresh adventure, the turning point could come this week.

Monday 16th

You may want to get your head down and concentrate on work or chores, but you could find that you're easily distracted, especially if there are lots of diversions and distractions. Give yourself a break by lining up some straightforward activities to tick off your to-do list.

Tuesday 17th

You may have to make a tough decision about your finances in the near future. This could mean cutting your losses or plugging a black hole down which your money has been disappearing. Deal with whatever's urgent in your life, but consider making money management your top priority.

Wednesday 18th

A financial issue might turn in your favour today as your planet Mercury turns direct in your money zone. This may coincide with new information or the news you've been waiting for. You could be able to close the door on a challenging time.

Thursday 19th

You may now receive a compliment or find the support or advice you've been looking for. Team up with other people in your life, personally and professionally. As a Gemini, you're at your best when you have a wide network of friends and a varied social circle, so reach out.

Friday 20th

There's now less emphasis on Capricorn, the serious, dutiful star sign, and more emphasis on freedom-loving Aquarius. This means that you're likely to be feeling sociable and lively, and once the Sun lights up air sign Aquarius, you're going to be fizzing with fun and creativity.

Saturday 21st

Use today's new moon to set your intentions. This is the right time to draw up your resolutions for 2023, so put your ideas to good use and line up activities to look forward to. Seeds can be sown concerning travel and study.

Sunday 22nd

Wherever you want to explore life, your astrology is calling you forth. After a period where money matters may have dominated, concerns about what you own and earn may be alleviated. Think about a travel or study plan.

Monday 23rd

Start the week by problem-solving and find a solution to an ongoing issue. If you're seeking new experiences in life, you should get serious about them by drawing up a plan. Wishing your life away won't bring you fulfilment.

Tuesday 24th

If you've not been feeling in tune with your work or vocation recently, you might be itching for a change. It's never easy when your personal and professional goals are out of alignment. Rather than getting frustrated, concentrate on what is working well.

Wednesday 25th

This is a great time to use your brilliant brain to learn more. If you're studying or about to take a test or exam, the stars are on your side. Your fantasy world could be active now, so put this to good use by drawing up a new cosmic wish list.

Thursday 26th

If you've been making new friends over the last eight months or so, you're in tune with your stars. Your close connections can benefit your life in many different ways right now. This is where good fortune and opportunity lie, so continue to focus on your friendships and connections.

Friday 27th

The right partnership may benefit your career, so look out for someone who steps into your life today. Working alongside inspirational and creative types can boost your progress. This is your opportunity to find a path that's meaningful and makes a difference in other people's lives.

Saturday 28th

If you want to have some time out this weekend, it's a good moment to do so. You might catch up on sleep or indulge in some important rest and relaxation. Give yourself time to dream about your future and consider lining up some new and exciting adventures.

Sunday 29th

Try not to let your mind run away with you today. If you're typical of your star sign, there's a hyperactive side to your nature that sometimes causes you to overthink things. Meditation could help to calm your nerves. Alternatively, distract yourself from worrying by getting active.

Monday 30th

An idea that first cropped up in mid-December is worth reinvestigating today, especially if it's about using online technology to boost your financial knowledge. With the moon in Gemini, you're going to be buzzing with exciting and innovative ideas today.

Tuesday 31st

It's a positive end to the first month of the year, so you're right to be proactive and ambitious. Focus on your personal goals and aims, as well as your image and your profile. Boost your physical fitness and build up your strength. It could be a great day to commit to joining a gym.

FEBRUARY

·····················

Wednesday 1st
You may find that you float your way through the day and are more dreamy than productive as a result. The energy shifts at midday, when you should be more ready to take on the world and make things happen. Rather than focusing on the here and now, start to think about the future and plan your next steps.

Thursday 2nd
If there's someone you think could help with your career or vocational goals, reach out to them today. It's usually easier to make progress when you have the right people on your side. Use your communication skills to your advantage.

Friday 3rd
You might be coming towards the end of something that has needed your attention for a while, and if so, you should feel pleased with yourself. Think carefully before leaping into a new agreement. Moving forward, freedom could be a huge factor.

Saturday 4th
Full moon vibes light up your social life. This is about meeting new people, so it could be good to say yes to a party or last-minute invitation that comes your way. If your plans change suddenly, you might have no option but to be flexible.

Sunday 5th

It's a full moon weekend, which can be good for studying and teaching. Know where you shine bright in life and show off your skills and talents. This is your time to step up and share your knowledge with others.

Monday 6th

You may find it challenging to get hold of the right people today. Alternatively, someone might say no to your request leaving you disappointed. Shrug off any setbacks and resolve to try again another day. A quiet evening at home will help to soothe your ego.

Tuesday 7th

It's a day for resting rather than for business. Perhaps you can shift things around so you're working from home. You need strong foundations in your life now. Go for a walk in nature, cook or get crafty. If arguments flare up this evening, try to calm things down.

Wednesday 8th

Look out for a person who has an alternative viewpoint or a different way of looking at life. If this is someone you work with, their ideas could prove to be a revelation. Consider using your charm to get on the right side of someone in a position of power.

Thursday 9th

Dealing with an issue first thing should put a spring in your step and leave you free to turn your attention to pleasure and enjoyment. Even if you're at work, there's a flirtatious vibe. Be first in the queue to have some fun.

Friday 10th

Try to close the door on a matter that's been dragging on over the last few months. Make a final decision today, then try to cut your losses and move on. If you would like to be more ambitious, give yourself a good talking to.

Saturday 11th

Your planet Mercury is on the move this weekend, and freedom is the buzzword. You might be heading off on your travels or be taking part in a workshop or educational course. It's a good time to expand your horizons and plan an adventure for the year ahead.

Sunday 12th

You may be keen to get away or go somewhere completely different today. A change can be as good as a rest, so your brain is primed and ready to take in new information during what is a positive period to improve your knowledge or learn a new skill.

Monday 13th

You might find it hard to concentrate today. It helps to remember that you're a multitasker at heart, so you may find it easier to get more done when you have different jobs or tasks on the go, rather than just the one project. Hang in there and keep going.

Tuesday 14th

The moon is in your relationship zone on Valentine's Day, so try to make it a special one. Even if you're single, it's a good day to attend a party or get-together. Love and friendship are linked, so try to make the most of your personal opportunities and close connections.

Wednesday 15th

The key to success is to do what you love and follow your passion, so trust your feelings and go with the flow. It may help to use images to inspire you regarding your future path. Be creative and allow yourself to dream.

Thursday 16th

If you're typical of your star sign, you like to live in the present, so you may not always be great at drawing up long-term plans. Today's astrology is urging you to think about the future, so get definite about a travel or study option. If you want to change your future path, dig deep.

Friday 17th

It's likely to be a steady end to the working week. You may want to delve into more unusual topics today, perhaps by exploring a therapeutic path. You might also find that you're fascinated by the workings of the mind or be on a personal development mission.

Saturday 18th

It's a great weekend to learn to quieten your mind and develop your creative side. Ideas you come up with over the next few weeks could significantly improve your life moving forward. Turn your attention to where you're heading in life and why.

Sunday 19th

You're likely to be raring to go and full of great ideas today. Use technology to learn more about whether you want to gain new qualifications, and reach out to people who may already be knowledgeable in the areas you're interested in.

Monday 20th

A new moon in your career zone is ideal for initiating a project or business idea. If you're starting something new, you're in tune with your stars. When you feel good about your life, this rubs off on other people.

Tuesday 21st

There may be some frustration today, especially if plans don't work out. It might feel like a Mercury retrograde phase even though it's not. Expect the unexpected and be flexible and adaptable. Sometimes it's the journey rather than the destination that matters.

Wednesday 22nd

If you are a sociable Gemini, lucky opportunities are linked to your friendships and group activities. This is especially true for you now and over the next couple of weeks. Getting in with the right crowd could boost your potential.

Thursday 23rd

Line up some fun and inspirational activities today, either at work or socially. You'll often be at your best when you're surrounded by other people and you're firing off each other's high-vibe energy. Consider joining a group, club or society.

Friday 24th

You might want to slow things down today, especially if you've been racing through life recently. Trying to catch up with everyone and keep other people happy can be exhausting in the long run. Consider booking a massage or some pampering. Take care of yourself.

Saturday 25th

You may enjoy yourself more this weekend when you're on your own. Take some time out to be creative, and try some hands-on activities like cooking, art or gardening. This will encourage your ideas to flow.

Sunday 26th

If you're feeling tired or low on energy, don't fight it. Give in to your mood and line up a quiet day. Sometimes you need to stop completely to allow your mind time to settle. You should sense a positive shift in energy this evening.

Monday 27th

If the weekend provided you with some rest and retreat, you'll be firing on all cylinders and ready to get back out into the world today. It's a good day to use your contacts to make new connections, both personally and professionally. Put your networking skills to good use.

· · · · · · · · · · · · · · · · · ·

Tuesday 28th

As an air sign, you're likely to be good at processing information. This is because you make sense of things through your interactions with other people. Bear this in mind as you decide what you want and where you're heading today.

MARCH

· · · · · · · · · · · · · · · · ·

Wednesday 1st

Your emotional needs are likely to feel important right now, so you might enjoy food shopping or buying items that make you feel comfortable and cosy. You might receive good news and decide to celebrate later on.

Thursday 2nd

When planets are at the peak of your horoscope, it's about finding your place in the world and considering the bigger picture. You might be busy today, especially if you have meetings or interviews lined up. It's a good time to trust your intuition, so do what feels right.

Friday 3rd

If a friend of yours has some good news to share, make sure you celebrate together properly. This evening looks great for getting a new group of people together. If you've recently joined a club or society, this could prove to be an exceptionally lucky time for you.

Saturday 4th

You may have friends staying over this weekend, or you might be catching up with a good friend who's visiting from abroad. Expand your social circle and get to know new people. A late change of plan could work out to your advantage, so be spontaneous and great change with a smile.

Sunday 5th

If you're a typical Gemini, you can talk to almost anyone. This weekend is great for getting to know the neighbours better or for joining in with a community event. You might be the one organising a get-together, or someone else could ask you to take on a leading role and make a speech.

Monday 6th

This week, look closely at the work/life balance and trust your instincts about what to do about it. There's a full moon tomorrow, so family connections will be important. This isn't the time to let other people hold you back, however much you care about them. Be bold.

Tuesday 7th

If you're looking for a new job or a promotion, be proactive. If you're involved in a big project, expect it to be full-on now. Full moons are often a time of completion or culmination and can coincide with achievement. The focus should be on the future and your long-term goals.

Wednesday 8th

You or someone in your family may step into a more senior role this week. If so, it could mean more duty and responsibility for everyone involved. If you hear about a family member who loses their job, it's important that everyone rallies around them. Encourage others to get in touch.

Thursday 9th

If the start of the week has been overly busy, you'll be ready to let your hair down and have some fun. If your social scene is lively and vibrant, make the most of it. Work your connections and spend time with other people.

Friday 10th

A new romance or love affair could become complicated today, especially if you find that anything goes regarding love and relationships. Alternatively, you might be watching a good friend play a risky love game.

Saturday 11th

The feel-good vibes continue into the weekend, so ensure you have some top entertainment lined up. Love and friendship might remain complex, but enjoy yourself nonetheless. Don't dismiss your work or responsibilities, especially if you know you need to up your game over the next few weeks.

Sunday 12th

Trust your intuition around work issues. If someone's reached out to you this weekend, follow up on this. A decision to take an unusual direction in your career path could pay off for you. Shoot off some emails and be spontaneous in your approach.

Monday 13th

Take care not to get on the wrong side of someone you work with. Building good relations will be important over the next couple of years, so it's wise to maintain a good reputation. If your partner's going through a tough time, be there for them.

. . . .

Tuesday 14th

You may feel disillusioned with where you're heading today or realise you don't have the support you want to further your plans. If in doubt, go with the flow and trust yourself, but keep the big moves up your sleeve. Remember that you don't have to divulge everything to everyone.

Wednesday 15th

Today's astrology feels creative and inspirational. It's a promising day if you work in an artistic field or a caring industry. However, if you're feeling unsure about your current career path, you could experience some confusion now.

Thursday 16th

If you're not on track with what you're doing, things could feel strange and disorienting today. If in doubt, go with the flow instead of wasting your energy getting angry about what's happening. If you're an artist or musician, this period could be inspirational.

Friday 17th

Love has a private or secretive theme today, so it's not a great time to mix business with pleasure. You might need to prove that you're on the ball at work and by stepping up to the next level. Be professional and try to keep your personal and professional lives separate.

Saturday 18th

This is a good moment to take a complete break from work, especially if it's been a confusing or disorienting time. Do something different or go somewhere you've never been before. If you catch up with a friend you haven't seen for a while, they may be able to offer a fresh perspective on your situation.

Sunday 19th

You may be getting itchy feet and want to see more of your social circle. If you're going through a busy patch at work, it might be time to find new ways to be spontaneous. It doesn't have to be about a major event; even grabbing a cup of coffee with a friend can make all the difference.

Monday 20th

The Sun's move into Aries heralds the equinox and the start of a new season. This lights up your friendship and group sector, which is where enjoyment lies. However, this doesn't mean that you can neglect your work. Get your head down and ensure you take your responsibilities seriously.

Tuesday 21st

Today's new moon highlights friendship and group activities in your horoscope. It's a wonderful day to reconnect with good friends, so consider reaching out on social media. If you've been thinking about networking or joining an online group, here's your cosmic opportunity.

Wednesday 22nd

When you have good friends by your side, it feels as if you can take on the world. If you're working alongside a friend or you're involved in a group venture with the people closest to you, your project could fly now.

Thursday 23rd

Today marks an epic move that could link back to events in 2008. It's not the end of this particular chapter yet, as you may have a few months to reconsider things. Wipe your hands clean or breathe a sigh of relief.

Friday 24th

You may be experiencing unrequited feelings or be lusting after someone who is unavailable. It might be wise to bide your time concerning love, even if you desire spontaneity and excitement. You may have to wait until the middle of next month to find out whether your affections can be made public.

Saturday 25th

Action planet Mars leaves your star sign today after an unusually long stay. You may feel less manic and more determined to boost your energy levels now. It's a good time to actively pursue beneficial activities.

Sunday 26th

There are some days when you feel comfortable in your skin, and this may be one of them. There's an easy flow between what you want and need, so you'll enjoy being around other people. Hang out and enjoy yourself.

Monday 27th

You might be building towards a big social event, perhaps a fundraiser or charity gala that you've helped to organise. Alternatively, there could be a party or social occasion that you're looking forward to. This is a good time for group activities, so consider joining in.

Tuesday 28th

If this proves to be your lucky day, make the most of it. You may become an influencer or meet a celebrity, while winning the work raffle or an invite into a select group of people are also possibilities. Whatever comes your way, puff out your chest with pride and say yes.

Wednesday 29th

It's a time when you're likely to care deeply about other people and, more importantly, want to show that you care. Support the people around you and consider getting involved with a charity event or good cause.

Thursday 30th

You may be aware of the divide between your personal and professional life today. It could be that, in your professional life, you're a model of responsibility and worthy of respect, while in your personal life, there are some weird things going on. Try to change the balance for the better.

Friday 31st

It's all about your connections today, whether you're at work, at home or being sociable. Think about doing something special with a group of friends. One friendship in particular is likely to be mutually supportive and a great boon for both of you.

APRIL
·················

Saturday 1st
You may have a connection that you're keeping secret for a
particular reason. If this is true, it might be better not to let
other people know, especially siblings or relatives. If you have
your reasons for this, that's justification enough.

Sunday 2nd
You may be pulled back towards the past today, whether you're
visiting your childhood home or meeting an elderly relative.
Try not to become overly morbid. It's a good day to sort out the
family finances or draw up a budget.

Monday 3rd
You may be entering a private phase now, perhaps because
you're keeping a secret or dealing with a hidden issue. Events
going on behind the scenes might force you to change your
mind about a trip away or decide to postpone a course of study.

Tuesday 4th
You might want to get back in touch with someone from your
past. This could be a romantic relationship or a person you
grew up with. Alternatively, you could decide to attempt to find
long lost family over the next couple of months.

Wednesday 5th

If you're working to a tight deadline, seek peace and quiet in your life and limit the noise. Do whatever's necessary to create the right working environment, even if it means limiting your social life or cancelling a leisure event.

Thursday 6th

Today's full moon highlights your relationships, so it's a good time to interact with someone dear to your heart. Reach out to your friends and find new ways to connect. This is especially important if your schedule is constantly changing.

Friday 7th

A tight work deadline could eat into your Easter weekend. If you're unable to delegate or negotiate more time, do what you can to keep on top of things. This evening is perfect for a night in with someone special.

Saturday 8th

You may have to spend some of today dealing with a work issue. Don't put off what you know needs to get done. You could come up with some new ideas, or you might make some progress with a home or family project.

Sunday 9th

If you haven't spent much time with your partner this weekend, try to get together this afternoon or evening. If one of you is working, you can still carve out some time to be together. Let other people in your life step in and take the lead.

Monday 10th

You may be ready for more interactions with other people today. Whether you're hanging out with a group of academics or a brainy friend, be open to learning and knowledge. Love and foreign cultures are connected, as are love and study.

Tuesday 11th

As Venus moves into Gemini, your love life could be elevated to a whole new level. If anyone's going to be penning romantic poetry or love letters, it's you. This is also a great time to look after yourself, to appreciate the beauty in the world and to seek enjoyment wherever you find it.

Wednesday 12th

Turn your attention to the serious business of life today and get on top of work and finances. It's a good time to deal with these key areas, especially as you'll feel better when you've ticked some important items off your to-do list. Try not to let your temper flare over money.

Thursday 13th

You may struggle to find time for a good friend today, especially if work beckons. If one friend is celebrating this week, you'll be keen arrange a date to meet. You may be diving deep into a new subject this evening.

Friday 14th

You might experience a disappointment today, especially if someone close lets you down. Try not to read too much into this and remember that sometimes people get busy. Consider keeping your personal and professional lives separate.

Saturday 15th

It's a perfect Saturday to meet up with friends for brunch or
a social get-together. You may be watching sport together, or
perhaps you all share a unique interest. Make the most of the
weekend and do something unusual and different.

Sunday 16th

You may be on a new path now, so be open to storytelling and
poetry, and allow music to be your muse. Explore the world of
art and beauty and allow it to restore a sense of purpose and
meaning within you. If work calls, do what you must.

Monday 17th

You might be juggling various roles at work today, and your
responsibilities could weigh heavily upon you. If you're a
creative type, dive into the artistic side of your work.

Tuesday 18th

A solar eclipse takes place in the early hours of Thursday
morning, and this means that people power is on the rise.
Even though you might want to do your own thing, right now
your focus should be on joining in, showing your support and
teaming up with others.

Wednesday 19th

You may want to drop everything to be there for a friend
who needs you today. Your protective nature will kick in, and
you're likely to be more than willing to step in to help. If so,
the experience could be powerful for both of you, and might
create a lasting bond.

Thursday 20th

Today's eclipse hints at an ending followed by a beginning. Perhaps you decide to leave a group, or you find that you're ready to say goodbye and move on from some aspect of your life. Letting go of a specific role can create space to embrace an exciting new activity.

Friday 21st

Your planet Mercury turns retrograde today. If someone leaves, it might be best to let them go. Think about getting rid of what's not working out in your life so that you can begin again. Take a step back to reassess what's happening or to nurse your feelings.

Saturday 22nd

You may feel as if you're having to put yourself back together after a tricky few days. Eclipse energy can be powerful, and the Sun's move into your hidden zone could provide a clue about what you need. Trust that the wheel of fortune will turn in your favour once again.

Sunday 23rd

Remember that you currently have Venus, one of the best planets, in your star sign. This is perfect for vibrant loving relationships and finding the positives in life. Keep your sense of humour strong and do more of what you love today.

Monday 24th

You might have to go back on an agreement if things aren't working out. Don't be afraid of speaking up and changing your mind. If you are doing well financially, it might be best to keep a tight hold of your money and avoid getting caught up in any crazy schemes.

Tuesday 25th

It's important to be sensible and realistic when it comes to money. Whether you're setting up a savings plan or working out a long-term budget, do your sums and prioritise your future security. This is even more important if you have people who rely on you.

Wednesday 26th

If your social life is changing, ask yourself whether this is the result of a conscious decision. Going out frequently can cost a lot of money over time and you might have to rein things in now, especially if you have a specific reason to spend less now.

Thursday 27th

You may not be the sort of person to spend too much time on your own, but that might be what you choose over the next couple of months. You could use this time to learn meditation or become absorbed in a course of study. Do what you know is right for you.

Friday 28th

You find that you're less keen to hang out with the crowd than usual. What is likely to get you out of the house, however, is the lure of love. A partnership or the promise of new love could bring you satisfaction.

Saturday 29th

Make time for a good friend today and do something cultural together. You could have a brilliant idea about how to make money or boost your finances. Think outside of the box and do something different. Consider all your options.

Sunday 30th

You deserve some chill out time, so put your feet up and take it easy today. If you're hanging out with your family, it might be better not to talk about work. It's a good day to reminisce and recall your memories together, both happy and sad.

MAY

. . . .

Monday 1st

Some of your plans or goals may have to be put on hold,
perhaps concerning travel or study. One dream may have
become outdated, or you might realise that there are too many
obstacles to overcome. Listen to your inner voice and look out
for the signposts that signal freedom.

Tuesday 2nd

If something hasn't worked out the way you hoped it would,
pick yourself up. It's a good day to look on the bright side of
things and find the positives in life's interventions. Focus on
simple pleasures before deciding what comes next.

Wednesday 3rd

You could be feeling wilful and want to splurge your money
just because you can. Think twice, however, before being
impulsive. It might be better to clear out your wardrobe or
clean your home instead. Try and appreciate what you have.

Thursday 4th

You're wise to slow down the pace of life today. Perhaps you
feel weighed down by a heavy workload that's proving stressful.
Learn from recent lessons and prioritise yourself whenever
possible. Love may prove elusive this evening.

Friday 5th

Today's lunar eclipse should highlight where change is necessary, both in your work or lifestyle. Focus on the basics of life and get these right before you start something new. When it comes to love, be honest about your feelings.

Saturday 6th

Create rules to live by that benefit you and consider adopting a new healthy habit. Be vigilant and prioritise yourself. Keeping fit and healthy will help you deal with any major change to your routine or working life.

Sunday 7th

As Venus moves into Cancer, it lights up your money zone, so there could be a positive change in your earnings. This is a promising sign that suggests you'll be better able to value your skills and talents. Perhaps you want to treat yourself or the ones you love.

Monday 8th

If your love life is going well, prioritise romance and relationships. It might be a Monday, but it's worth making a special effort this evening to let someone know how much you care. Not all your partnerships will be easy to navigate now, but do your best, especially at work.

Tuesday 9th

Focus on inner worth and transformation rather than what's happening out in the world. Try to recognise the power of your intuition and the importance of your mindset. The lively planetary vibe could lead to a moment of genius.

Wednesday 10th

You may have to return to a financial issue before too long. Today's stars could help you come up with new ideas around money, so take the time to think things through. You might surprise yourself with a clever solution.

Thursday 11th

The cosmic energy isn't settled, so your brain is likely to be overly active today, and you may find it harder than usual to still your busy and curious mind. Ideally, you'll have different plans or projects on the go, as this allows you to be more efficient than if you were focused solely on one task.

Friday 12th

Your planet Mercury remains in retreat this weekend and gives the illusion of moving backwards. Traditionally, this is a time to slow down, take a step back and look at your life from a fresh perspective. Find time to relax so that you can think about what comes next.

Saturday 13th

This is a good weekend to work alongside other people and help one another out. If you need a shot of inspiration, turn to friends who know how to motivate you. A role model could unlock the door to a more fulfilling career path.

Sunday 14th

Mercury turns direct tomorrow, making this is a powerful time to use your mind to good effect. Consider what you've learned over the last few weeks and decide who you need to contact and what you're going to set in motion. Revisit your past ideas.

Monday 15th

Mercury's change of direction today could bring new information to light that might help to resolve a personal issue. You may be creatively inspired and keen to explore a more artistic way of life, or you could decide to try to earn money from something you make or produce.

Tuesday 16th

You're entering a new chapter, so you have an opportunity to be introspective, work on inner peace and find happiness in solitude. Caring is important right now, whether this is for yourself or someone else.

Wednesday 17th

Today's stars are a reminder to stop and breathe, to take time out from life and to find inspiration away from work and everyday matters. Think about planning something magical and mysterious. Explore the universe.

Thursday 18th

It's an ideal day for a decluttering session: let go of what's no longer necessary or needed in your life. You might be transported back to the past and feel that things are coming full circle. Tend to your inner life as much as your social life.

Friday 19th

Today's new moon falls in the hidden sector of your horoscope and is a reminder to slow down, relax and unwind. Take some time out this weekend to be in nature and take a step back from the stresses of life. Aim for a healthy work/life balance.

Saturday 20th

Action planet Mars is on the move and enters your communication sector. There's probably lots to talk about right now, and this might fire you up. Some conversations might seem urgent, and it may be hard not to speak your mind.

Sunday 21st

The Sun's move into Gemini quickens up the pace of life, so you should be ready to get things moving; this can be a helpful shift if you've felt stuck or immobilised recently. Use your lively mind and don't worry if you have endless projects on the go, as this likely suits your flexible nature.

Monday 22nd

You may be caught up in a power game or a negative situation, and it might feel important to speak up. If you've been a witness to injustice recently, look for an opportunity to put things right.

Tuesday 23rd

It might be hard not to fan the flames of an ongoing debate, discussion or argument today. If there's a lot of passion flying around, you're likely to feel strongly about what's taking place. It's an ideal lunchtime to catch up with someone special.

Wednesday 24th

It might be hard to put an ongoing argument to bed, and this afternoon and evening may feel tempestuous once again. If someone has got you fired up, you'll likely be ready for action. Take a stand about an important neighbourhood or social issue.

Thursday 25th

This is a positive period for learning or studying something new. Put your Gemini curiosity to good use by getting involved with your local education centre or a community organisation. If you have a habit of putting your foot in it and saying the wrong thing, take your time today.

Friday 26th

Your mind should be firing on all cylinders right now, so you might find it hard to sleep or switch off. Try to channel any nervous energy into a productive outlet, whether you're coming up with new ideas or helping someone out.

Saturday 27th

If you've had an exceptionally busy week, schedule some downtime this weekend and plan to do as little as possible. You'll probably be happy chilling out at home, even if you're just catching up with some chores. This is the moment to do less, not more.

Sunday 28th

Life has a strange way of stepping in and slowing you down if don't do so yourself. Be aware of this possibility and pay close attention to your stress levels. If you know that you need a break, it might be a good idea to find a way to let go of some of your responsibilities.

Monday 29th

Check your calendar first thing today to ensure you haven't forgotten an appointment or meeting. If you're worried about the future, try not to overthink things today. Instead, focus on what's working in your life and reorient your mind to enjoy the present moment.

Tuesday 30th

It's a great day for making new friends and reaching out to other people. If you're typical of your star sign, you love to have a wide social circle, and it's a good time to boost this area of your life. Catch up with the ones you love and have some fun with your family.

Wednesday 31st

If you want to treat someone close to you, today might be a good day to do so. Any gesture that you make is likely to be well-received. Sometimes it's worth putting other people's needs before your own.

JUNE

. . . .

Thursday 1st

If you have a strict work deadline to meet, you might struggle over the next few days. Do what you can without causing yourself too much stress in the process. If it's appropriate, share your concerns with a boss or authority figure.

Friday 2nd

It's always wise to get a second opinion about an important issue. Try not to let any anxieties kick in, even if things feel particularly unsettled. A person in a position of influence could prove to be a great help and might help calm your nerves.

Saturday 3rd

Full moons are wonderful for celebration, so you might be out and about enjoying yourself this evening. If you're looking for love, consider reaching out and making new connections. Be at your sociable best.

Sunday 4th

Today's full moon highlights your relationship zone. Emotions are heightened during this time of drama and strong reactions. This doesn't mean that it's time to hide what you're feeling: it depends on how bold you are and whether you're ready to open your heart.

Monday 5th

Venus, the planet of love and relating, moves into your communication zone today, and this is your cue to express your true feelings. However, this may be easier said than done, depending on who you've fallen for. One relationship may prove to be off limits.

Tuesday 6th

You may be getting ready to send your ideas out into the world, but it's better to stay quiet for now. You'll be more productive if you remain grounded and take life slowly rather than getting caught up in escapades.

Wednesday 7th

This might be a tricky time for a relationship, especially if you're not in agreement with one another. For example, you might want to go away on holiday, but discover that your partner isn't keen. Notice where in life you're out of step but don't rush to find an answer. Decide which battles are worth fighting and when it's better to pull back.

Thursday 8th

You may get caught up in an argument today, perhaps because you have different opinions to another person or within a group of people. Try to let other people have their points of view, and you will find that they listen in return.

Friday 9th

It's a good time to turn your focus towards your career and future path, especially if you're seeking inspiration. It's easier to make steady progress when you're clear about where you're heading and why.

Saturday 10th

Money is an area that often requires caution. There may be a chance to end a contract or partnership that isn't working out, or perhaps you're dealing with a debt or inheritance. Do your best to ensure your money is secure.

Sunday 11th

Mercury, the planet of communication, enters your star sign today, so you should consider what it is you want to say, write or talk about. What ideas are you dreaming up? If you act fast, you might be able to resolve a personal issue. Put the past behind you and keep moving forward.

Monday 12th

You should find that you're more productive now, especially if you're working alongside people you get on with. You might be in the process of setting up a business with a good friend, or perhaps you're making an extra effort to get to know a person you see every day. Team up with others.

Tuesday 13th

Avoid an emotional situation by keeping money out of the equation, especially where friends are concerned. Proceed carefully, as a past misdemeanour could catch you out.

Wednesday 14th

If in doubt, say nothing. You're a Gemini, so you're likely to love talking and telling stories. However, it's worth stopping and counting to ten before opening your mouth. It might be best to avoid revealing everything.

Thursday 15th

If you're up against it at work, take a few deep breaths. You may feel like giving up, but try to dig deep and do what you can. Find someone that can support you and lean on them for help. Your friends will make you stronger.

Friday 16th

You should feel like you're back in the driving seat today and might be ready to make an important decision about your next steps. Your personal life may be more important to you than your professional status or reputation right now. Be honest about what's happening.

Saturday 17th

If things aren't working out for you, take a step back this weekend. It might help to talk to someone who knows you well, such as a good friend or relative. A new chapter is beginning tomorrow, and this could help you to decide what comes next. Put yourself and your needs first.

Sunday 18th

Today's new moon in Gemini is perfect to set your intentions, not only for next month but for the year ahead as well. Find time to work on your personal goals. Gemini is the sign of the writer, so take notes and make lists. Alternatively, phone a friend and talk things through.

Monday 19th

If you're having a career crisis or you're unsure what the future holds, this will feel unsettling. Events might happen that help you to see where you're ready to move on, but you should take your time if you can, as rushing into something new isn't necessarily wise. Try and find a compromise instead.

Tuesday 20th

You may be inspired to set off on a new journey, perhaps one that brings out your inner poet, musician or designer. Reassess what's important to you and ask whether you're satisfied with your vocation.

Wednesday 21st

Take a close look at money matters today and consider what you value most in life. It's a good time to prioritise your feelings of self-worth and validation. If you want someone to talk you up, ask one of your friends to remind you of your strengths and talents.

Thursday 22nd

If you're the type of Gemini who makes friends easily, your social skills will be on fire today. Make the most of your contacts and line up some exciting opportunities. Your passionate nature may extend to a romantic relationship, so use your communication skills.

Friday 23rd

Turn your attention towards your home and your family over the weekend, and take a closer look at family finances or consider some home improvements. Your security might matter to you now, but this doesn't mean you have to go it alone. Be part of a strong team.

Saturday 24th

Take some time to consider the life's bigger picture and where you're heading. If you're typical of your star sign, you enjoy living in the moment. However, you're wise to look to the future right now. May 2024 could be a significant turning point so work towards this.

Sunday 25th

You might be pulled in different directions today, and this is rarely a satisfying experience. It may be best to prioritise your home, family and personal life. If you feel disillusioned about your situation, try not to let your mind run away from you.

Monday 26th

Today's stars could be volatile, so make sure you think before you speak. You may be frustrated about something you read or hear, or perhaps transport lets you down. Try not to let external events get you down.

Tuesday 27th

The ideas you come up with and the conversations you have over the next two weeks could help improve your financial situation. Money will be more important for you from today, so think about getting to grips with finances, sending correspondence or lining up an important meeting.

Wednesday 28th

Show you mean business by getting on top of work and money matters. Engaging emotionally with life's events can help you stay on track, as doing so will give a deeper meaning or purpose to what you're doing.

Thursday 29th

Good things might start happening for you now, and you may discover a new sense of ambition and purpose. If you're going to be successful, you'll have to be disciplined and do what's necessary. This might mean playing by the rules and being nice to your boss.

Friday 30th

This is a positive time of year to notice how you come across to other people, so pay close attention to your image and profile. You might create a new website or rewrite your CV to make a good impression. Get on board with what's required and try to make steady progress.

JULY

Saturday 1st

Listen out for signs and synchronicities today. Something you hear or read could be the catalyst that sets you on a new and prosperous path. Your luck is often linked to past connections, so consider reaching out to a relative.

Sunday 2nd

Love relationships are often exciting, but are about to enter a complex period. You may get a hint of what this is about today, especially if someone else's behaviour is unusual or unexpected. It could be your love life that's about to take an interesting turn, or it could be someone else's.

Monday 3rd

Today's full moon highlights your money zone, so security is likely to be important to you now, both financially and emotionally. Consider your self-worth and rethink what money means to you. Use this cosmic opportunity to turn things around financially and get back on track with important money goals.

Tuesday 4th

If you have a long-term financial goal to aim for, it's easier to stay on track and keep tabs on how you're doing. If you're thinking about getting your finances in order, you're in tune with your stars. Planning is key.

Wednesday 5th

You may be planning a holiday or getting ready to take some time off work. Even if things have been busy recently, you still need a break and time away from the job. You might consider a sabbatical or holiday in the second half of 2024.

Thursday 6th

It may be easier to plan a trip away on your own rather than getting too involved with what other people want. Don't let a partner's plans hold you back, and be wary if you're organising a family trip; trying to cater for too many people could turn into a logistical nightmare.

Friday 7th

Use your wily Gemini ways to act fast today. Communicate well, find out who's on your side and line up key allies to support what you want to do. It's a good time to explore your options and embrace the new things in your life, especially regarding relationships, work and money.

Saturday 8th

Having a varied lifestyle suits your flexible nature, and this side of your personality will come to the fore this weekend. Your skills and expertise might be called upon today, so consider where you can be helpful and make an impact.

Sunday 9th

You may need something to lose yourself in now, whether it's a good book, a relationship or a creative project. Try not to be disappointed or disillusioned with where you're heading in life. There's an illusory feel to your stars now, so focus on what's reality rather than what's fantasy.

Monday 10th

You may have to do something that feels difficult or that you would prefer to put off, perhaps involving a group activity or a social venture. Think carefully before saying yes. Concentrate on your personal long-term goals, especially around home, family and money matters.

Tuesday 11th

You should find yourself in a period of preparation or self-exploration. You may discover more about who you are as you get ready for a new chapter in your life that begins next year. If you have big plans, ensure you have a your route planned out.

Wednesday 12th

It promises to be a lively couple of weeks, so it's time to brainstorm, share ideas and speak up. If you're a typical Gemini, you're likely to be a brilliant linguist, so learning a new language would be perfect now.

Thursday 13th

There might be times during this period when you go against the status quo or you're out of step with what everyone else wants. As long as you're not overly bothered by other people's opinions, it's an ideal time to walk your own path and be true to who you are.

Friday 14th

Learn to trust yourself and your intuition. When the moon is in your star sign, it's important to put yourself first and pay close attention to your needs. What do you want more of, and what do you want less of? Think carefully before acting.

Saturday 15th

Create some space in your life today for daydreaming and pondering. Be by the sea or go for a walk by a lake or river. When you have nothing to do, your creative juices start flowing. Money is one area that may require your attention.

Sunday 16th

Ensure that you have trustworthy individuals in your life. Getting the right boss or expert on your side could be helpful in more ways than one. Sometimes it's hard to recognise your own skills or talents, and this is where someone else can step in and guide you.

Monday 17th

Today's new moon may help you to make an important decision around money. Are you saving up for something special or chasing money owed? Alternatively, do you want to do things differently regarding money matters? Set new intentions in place and be cash savvy.

Tuesday 18th

Notice who's on your side when it comes to money and earnings, and consider where you can ask for support. Look at what's not working out and consider where you may need to let something go to improve your financial situation.

Wednesday 19th

It's a brilliant day for ideas, brainstorming and communication in general. You may be more confident about what you're doing, or perhaps you enjoy being the one in charge. Try to tick as many items off your to-do list as possible. Get busy.

Thursday 20th

Ensure you shine brightly at work today. Show off your skills and try to impress the boss. Home and family matters could cause potential sticking points, and it's here where you may have to make a tough decision, especially if your plans impact other people's lives.

Friday 21st

Your home and family life might be tricky until the end of August. You may have the builders in, or perhaps your living situation has changed. Whatever your personal issue, be patient and know that things should get better before long.

Saturday 22nd

This is not the time to avoid money matters. Get the right people on your side and do what you can to secure your future. Be knowledgeable rather than scared about finance. The more you know, the easier it is to make wise decisions.

Sunday 23rd

Venus turns retrograde in your communication zone today, and this is about speaking up and breaking the silence. If you're a chatty Gemini, however, sometimes it can serve you well not to reveal everything you're thinking. Keep some things private.

Monday 24th

The Venus retrograde phase favours silence and introspection. If this leads to an issue with a sibling or neighbour, be there for them and step in to help where you can. It's always good to help others wherever possible.

Tuesday 25th

If you have a lot to do today, it's worth getting up early. You may choose to spend time with someone you love before work. The early bird catches the worm today. Things might go downhill later, so try to pace yourself if possible.

Wednesday 26th

If you're a typical Gemini, you might prefer multitasking. However, your usual approach might not work for you today, especially if you're chasing a deadline or trying to impress the boss, so consider focusing on one thing at a time. Keep your eye firmly fixed on your chosen goal.

Thursday 27th

If you sense that someone close would benefit from a conversation, it's an excellent day to reach out. A romantic upset could cause a dip in mood. Alternatively, you may want to reconnect with someone from your past that you haven't seen in a long time.

Friday 28th

Mercury's move into Virgo highlights your home and family zone, so pay close attention to these areas of your life. Think about what you need to attend to and who requires your attention. It's always good to get organised at home.

Saturday 29th

Close relationships are under the cosmic spotlight today. You may be feeling romantic and wistful if you're thinking about someone close. This might concern an unrequited love, or you could be remembering someone you used to love. Reach out this evening.

Sunday 30th

Crack on with household chores and domestic matters. You can get a lot done if you apply yourself, especially if your family are able to help you. Alternatively, you might step in to assist a parent or elderly neighbour.

Monday 31st

If you want to raise money for something special, today's a great day to do so. You might be fundraising or have an entrepreneurial idea that you want to make progress with. Use technology to your advantage and don't be shy about coming forward. A strong sense of self-belief will help.

AUGUST

· · · · · · · · · · · · · · · · ·

Tuesday 1st

Today's full moon highlights travel and study matters in your horoscope. Traditionally, this is a positive full moon to plan or set off on a holiday. However, your stars are pulling you back close to home, perhaps because you have priorities beyond holidays and fun. Do what's right for you.

Wednesday 2nd

You might be on the defensive at work, especially if you can't get time off to do what you want. Duty and responsibility could be big themes for you this year, especially when it comes to your career. You may be more aware of how these things hold you back now rather than how they propel you forward.

Thursday 3rd

You may be up against it today, especially if you have a difficult boss. Sometimes life's challenges are easier to deal with, but sometimes things are more difficult, and this may be one of those difficult days. Do what you can without bending over backwards for other people.

Friday 4th

Don't take a bad mood out on your loved ones. Instead, dream up a cosmic wish list and seek inspiration. Use visuals to inspire you at work or watch a film that stirs your imagination. It's a good time to reinvent yourself at work.

Saturday 5th

Now is the time to put work concerns to one side and spend time with your friends. Socialise and have some fun with your favourite people. This weekend is perfect for an exciting adventure or something new.

Sunday 6th

There's a feel-good vibe to your weekend stars. Your astrology is encouraging you to make friends and meet up with your favourite people. A community event could be ideal, especially if you can let your hair down and have fun. Kick back and enjoy yourself today.

Monday 7th

Yesterday's feel-good vibes could leak into the working week, and this may be a good thing. The more positive you are and the happier you feel, the more this could rub off on your colleagues, and this could help improve your work situation. You may begin to tire as the day goes on.

Tuesday 8th

You might have to slow the pace today, especially if you're tired or low on energy. You might be investing time in an online project that's grabbed your interest. If you're studying or researching, you're in tune with your stars.

Wednesday 9th

Someone close may let you down today, forcing you to change your schedule. Be flexible and don't take on more than you're comfortable with. The reappearance of an old flame could be both exciting and unsettling. Try not to let your personal life interfere with your work.

. . . .

Thursday 10th

If you're dealing with a financial issue, you should make steady progress today, as it's a good time to discuss money matters. Focus first on creating strong foundations for yourself and your family, then consider how you want to expand your own life.

Friday 11th

If you're seeking help, reach out to someone you've turned to previously, such as a colleague or a good listener. You might have to outsource some of what you're doing if you find that you're too busy.

Saturday 12th

You may feel an urge to tackle some of the big issues in your life today. Pay close attention and don't attempt to wing it when it comes to work and money. Make a long-term plan and be determined to see it through to completion.

Sunday 13th

Love planet Venus unites with the Sun, making this an ideal day to reach out to someone close, perhaps from your past. Find someone with whom you have a meaningful connection. What they have to say could prove useful in the future.

Monday 14th

It's not worth letting a financial issue become a big resentment today. Your stars look great for chatter, gossip and fun. Make new connections with people, enjoy yourself and spread happiness out in the world.

Tuesday 15th

If you're studying, reading or writing, things may take way longer than you expect today. This might be because you're fascinated by what you discover, or because you keep going off on tangents to find out more. What you're learning now could prove helpful to you in a new career.

Wednesday 16th

Use your communication skills and negotiate well. Today's new moon means that it's a good day to seek help. What you have to say could appeal to other people, although you may upset someone in the process. Don't let that stop you.

Thursday 17th

Your stars suggest a clash of conflicting ideas. You might want to make a stand and find that doing so makes you unpopular. Stand firm and be true to your principles. You can't please everyone all the time.

Friday 18th

You might not want to be sensible as you head towards the weekend, and that's not necessarily a bad thing. You may no longer be willing to put up with certain restrictions or feel hard done by. There's forward momentum in your astrology now, so go with it.

Saturday 19th

Any issues at home or within your family could flare up first thing. You might be worried about someone close to you. Things should improve from lunchtime onwards, especially if you know exactly what to say to sort things out. Spend quality time with your family.

Sunday 20th

It's a lovely day for chilling out with your friends and loved ones. There's a gentle vibe and a willingness to share positive feelings today. The more you benefit other people's lives, the more benefits you receive in return.

Monday 21st

This is a lively time of year when negotiations, talks and deals are prominent. You might be discussing a property deal, investments or an inheritance. Join forces with a partner on a project or sort out a personal issue together.

Tuesday 22nd

There's a clear divide between work and family today, and the pressures of juggling the work/life balance may feel overwhelming. Be wary of who you trust and don't assume that everyone's got your back. Any family issues that have bothered you previously could re-emerge now.

Wednesday 23rd

Your planet Mercury turns retrograde today, and this is your cosmic cue to back off and slow the pace. Put off any major decisions until Mercury turns direct in mid-September. Give yourself time to think about new developments relating to any important family matters.

Thursday 24th

Ensure your money is safe and aim to strengthen both your foundations and financial security. Don't let anyone push you into making a decision you're not happy with. Dig your heels in firmly and do what's right for you.

Friday 25th

This is a good day to broach a difficult subject with your family, so long as you are firm in your communications. It's a wonderful time for love, but don't make it all about your personal or family issues.

Saturday 26th

There may be a lot to deal with right now, but keep pushing for what you want regarding your future path and personal goals. Be determined to work out how to overcome any boundaries. Harness the strong planetary energy.

Sunday 27th

Passion planet Mars enters Libra and your romance zone today. If you're looking for love, it's a good time to up your game over the next few weeks. You're likely to appreciate more fun and want to be sociable or engage in leisure activities.

Monday 28th

It might be best to deal with serious matters before changing the record and focusing on how you can broaden your horizons moving forward. If you haven't been able to take a proper holiday this summer, it could be time to plan ahead.

Tuesday 29th

Doing something spontaneous and impulsive could pay off for you today, such as booking a holiday or getting back in touch with someone from your past. Whatever you do, make sure you have a good backup plan, as things could change again before too long.

Wednesday 30th

Be patient, tolerant and flexible while Mercury is moving slowly. Be aware that things could be changeable until mid-September. As Venus, the planet of relating, is also retrograde, you may find that you need to rethink your plans concerning your siblings and neighbours.

Thursday 31st

Things could peak today as an emotional full moon cuts across the foundations of your horoscope. There may be a clear divide between work and family, or the pressures of juggling the work/life balance might feel overwhelming. Listen to your intuition and trust your insights.

SEPTEMBER

· · · · · · · · · · · · · · · · ·

Friday 1st

It may be hard to keep your focus today, especially if your sights are already set on the weekend's events. Creative work may suit you best. Tempers might fray this evening, either if you're the one who's upset or you're consoling a good friend.

Saturday 2nd

It's a lovely weekend for being sociable and catching up with your favourite people. You're one of the outgoing air signs, so you're likely to be more than happy if you have numerous events and get-togethers lined up. Love is in the ascendancy, so it's a great day for a first date.

Sunday 3rd

The days after a full moon are ideal for releasing energy and letting go, so you may be discarding household items or releasing pent up emotions. Give in to your feelings and follow your heart. Do what feels right today rather than what you think you should be doing.

Monday 4th

Love planet Venus turns direct today, so if you want to leap in and make things happen, this is an ideal time to do so. Take the initiative and lead the way. There's a possibility that you might choose to let go of an unrequited love.

Tuesday 5th

Don't take too much on today. A theme of secrets is emerging, so you may have to deal with an issue that you wanted to keep private. You might struggle to let go of the past or be caught in the impossibility of a long-standing problem. Be kind to yourself, as this will help to improve things.

Wednesday 6th

This is a good day to prioritise quality family time or to visit someone from your past. It's a perfect opportunity to deepen your close connections, especially with the people in your life that you've known for years. Trust your intuition and line up an intimate and meaningful conversation.

Thursday 7th

The moon is in your star sign, so do more of what you love today. Put yourself and your needs first. You might need to seek inspiration at work, especially if you find that your mind wanders a lot. Give in to daydreaming and see how far your imagination can take you.

Friday 8th

Today's stars are about togetherness, caring for the ones you love and feeling appreciated in return. You may receive an unexpected gift or want to reach out and help someone close. If you sense a heart-to-heart would benefit a family member, it's best to speak up.

Saturday 9th

If you can come up with new ways to help others, you may discover that you receive help in return. This is a good moment for collaboration, so make the most of it. If you're planning a big event or celebration, there may be good news this evening.

Sunday 10th

You might find that you come up with a creative way of resolving an ongoing dilemma today. Brainstorm with your family and don't be nervous about discussing difficult topics. Consider calling a sibling or relative this evening.

Monday 11th

You'll be buzzing today if you hear relationship news or you're meeting exciting people. Make the most of your people skills, both personally and professionally. Even though it's a Monday, you may have a good reason to stay up late tonight.

Tuesday 12th

Technology could prove to be an issue today, as is often the case when Mercury is retrograde. Double-check everything and make sure that you save any documents you're working on. It's better to meet with someone in person rather than online.

Wednesday 13th

The flow of earth sign energy this week highlights your foundations as well as your money and work. You might feel held back or not know where you're heading, but don't let that stop you from planning your next steps. Keep on track with your long-term goals.

Thursday 14th

The end of this week is a positive period to connect with family members or to have a conversation with your flatmates. It's a time when you might be able to communicate well and get things done. A significant turning point in the key areas of home and family is on the way.

Friday 15th

Today's new moon in Virgo highlights home and family matters, as well as your past and where you come from. Virgo is an efficient star sign, so consider what needs doing at home and draw up a plan of action. As Mercury turns direct, you should experience a positive turn-around.

Saturday 16th

If you're dealing with a money matter, you may find that you make swift progress now. It's a good weekend to discuss financial issues. Aim to create strong foundations in your life. When you have a strong base, you can fly high.

Sunday 17th

Restore balance in your life, especially if there's tension between you and someone close. When you're in a good mood and feeling cheerful, this rubs off on other people. Be uplifting, compliment someone you love and reach out to other people.

Monday 18th

Turn your attention away from your personal life and get on with the job at hand. If you've taken your eye off the ball at work recently, it's important to show you mean business by getting back on track.

Tuesday 19th

Acknowledge if there's someone you're worried about at the moment and resolve to be in touch with the right people this evening or at the weekend. Your personal life could intrude on your work today, so you may be finding it hard to concentrate. Try to aim for a healthy work/life balance.

Wednesday 20th

Dig deep to find out more about a job or contract. How long will it last, and what are your prospects? Keep your options open and look at the alternatives. Your family could provide the solution to an ongoing issue.

Thursday 21st

Get other people on your side before dealing with a home or family matter. Being honest about what's happening in your personal life could deepen the bond between you and someone close. Prioritise your love life.

Friday 22nd

You may keep missing someone who you're trying to connect with. Don't give up and know that you'll be able to speak with them when the time is right. If you're worried about a financial issue, don't be on your own. Being around other people will help to lighten your mood.

Saturday 23rd

The Sun enters Libra and your romance and creativity zone today. When planets are in your element, you should find that your spirits rise and that anything feels possible. Put the focus on play and do more of what you love.

Sunday 24th

Libra rules not only romance but also creative projects and entertainment. Actively engage with these areas of your life now. It's important to focus on being optimistic now, so put your energy into the things that are working out for you.

. . . .

Monday 25th

The stars suggest you have an important role to play today, perhaps within your family or concerning people close to you. Others will be looking to you to make things harmonious or for help with a specific issue.

Tuesday 26th

There may be someone in your life who's hard to pin down at the moment. This could be a love interest, a person you'd like to get to know better or a relative who's being uncooperative. This weekend's full moon could reveal more.

Wednesday 27th

If you work hard over the next couple of days, you will find that you're pleased that you did so. It's a good day for being productive and ticking items off your to-do list. You should feel a welcome sense of achievement.

Thursday 28th

If you're planning on working at home, this may not be wise today. There could be too many distractions, so it might be easier to concentrate if you're in the office or have a quiet space to work in. You may not be overly confident about what you're doing, but don't put yourself down.

Friday 29th

Today's full moon has a social vibe. On the one hand, it's about romance and creativity, but on the other hand, friendship and group activities are important now. This full moon phase is a good time to get the answers you want or need.

Saturday 30th

If you are able to deal with a home or family-related issue quickly, you can get on with the more important business of enjoying yourself. Something important could be completed in the next few days. Think about making time to see your best friend this afternoon.

OCTOBER

Sunday 1st

Slow down and catch up on the things you haven't had time for. If you've been putting things off, you'll feel better once you've done them. Make sure you get enough sleep and recharge yourself. Make time to relax and nurture yourself.

Monday 2nd

Try not to fall prey to fear or doubt today and be proactive instead. You may have to broach an important subject to get things moving in the right direction. Keep coming back to the basics, use your common sense and focus on the facts. It's always best to have all the information.

Tuesday 3rd

You might experience a surge of energy today, especially if you're connecting with family members or completing a domestic project. Try to finalise things and bring an end to a long-drawn-out process.

Wednesday 4th

Consider where you need to restore balance and harmony in your life and prioritise fun and socialising. If love sweeps into your life today, romance could be a welcome escape from more mundane issues. A new, easier chapter may be about to begin.

Thursday 5th

Things should feel lighter for you from today onwards, and this is because your planet Mercury moves into Libra, your fellow air sign. You will start to make sense of recent events now, but you may need to step away from an important issue.

Friday 6th

You might receive a gift or an offer of help today. Someone else may take on a protective role, and you could benefit from their generosity. This is a good day to enjoy a romantic date or some time with your family.

Saturday 7th

Try not to give yourself a hard time if things aren't working out for you concerning a creative or artistic project. It could be one of those weekends where you experience a disappointment, and this may not be the end of the story. Other people's emotions could have an impact on your state of mind.

Sunday 8th

Proceed cautiously, especially if you're caught up in a difficult dynamic with someone close. While you may often try to fix things if they go wrong, it might be best to try a different response now. Sometimes it helps to let other people deal with their own issues. Be around someone who lifts your spirits.

Monday 9th

If there's a situation in your life that's difficult to manage, it may be best to get a third party involved. Someone in your family may be able to step in and help if you're in a tricky spot.

Tuesday 10th

If someone in your family is going through a big negative change, be there for them as best you can. You might not have the right words to help, but sometimes all that's required is a hug or some emotional support. It's a good idea to get the whole family on board.

Wednesday 11th

Get the right people on your side today and line up some expert advice. You don't have to go it alone, whatever your current situation. Look for a step-by-step solution to a problem and don't ignore what's happening.

Thursday 12th

Action planet Mars is a positive influence in your work and health zone right now, so you might choose to get fit, apply for a job or take steps to organise your time better. If you've got a lot going on, this is a good week to learn when to say no and how best to create a healthy work/life balance.

Friday 13th

Focus your attention on your work and aim to create strong foundations in your life. If there's a financial reason for working hard or taking on extra overtime, this may be a good idea. Overhaul your fitness routine this weekend and consider joining a new exercise group.

Saturday 14th

Today's solar eclipse could make for a dramatic and exciting time. Be open to the unexpected and willing to take a chance. The eclipse highlights romance, creative projects, entertainment and fun. Stay safe but consider a bold move.

Sunday 15th

You may have a pressing responsibility that's taking up your time and energy at the moment. If you had to disappoint someone in your life yesterday, think about letting them know that you're sorry. Whatever the situation, it's always important to ensure that your loved ones understand what's going on.

Monday 16th

When engaging in self-improvement, be careful not to go over the top. Try not to get carried away today and avoid becoming obsessive if your work or your health are out of balance. Rather than trying to fix things immediately, it's a good idea to start by calming your mind.

Tuesday 17th

When you transform your inner state, this can have a positive effect on what's happening externally. Focus on your inner self and try to work to change your mindset. Doing so could help you to deal with a heavy workload more easily.

Wednesday 18th

You may not be able to see as much of a loved one as you would like right now. Perhaps your partner is going through a busy period with their work and career. Alternatively, they might be visiting family or stepping in to help elderly parents. Keep in touch without appearing needy.

Thursday 19th

Try to put the past behind you and don't let old emotions get in the way of your life in the present day. This evening is perfect for hooking up with a lover or enjoying a new romance.

Friday 20th

If you've been involved in any kind of triangle situation recently, let someone know what's important to you and that you won't be swayed by anyone else's opinion. You might need to end a friendship that's not working out.

Saturday 21st

Try not to get too obsessed about a love relationship or an ongoing issue with someone close to you. At the same time, it's important to step in and speak up if you feel that you need to. If you're unable to see the ones you love, try to discover the reasons behind this.

Sunday 22nd

It might be best to try and steer clear of any emotional issues right now. Mercury's move into Scorpio today highlights your lifestyle and health zone, and this serves as a reminder to monitor your stress levels carefully. A new phase at work may be about to begin, so you spend time today preparing for a new role.

Monday 23rd

If you're looking for work, the Sun's move into Scorpio should provide you with new momentum, and doors could begin to open. Deepen your connections with colleagues and people who can help you professionally. The closer your bond, the more successful you will be.

Tuesday 24th

Your health is under the cosmic spotlight, so consider your routine and what works best for you. If you want to begin a new form of exercise or take on a healthy habit, this is the perfect time to do so. You might find that it's easier for you to be disciplined when you're being sociable as well.

Wednesday 25th

This is a good day to lean on others, so ensure that you have strong bonds at home and within your family. If a personal issue gets in the way of your working life, this could have a detrimental effect on your status and reputation.

Thursday 26th

If you're a typical Gemini, you're likely to have good communication skills, which will help you to fake it until you make it. If you can keep up the facade a while longer, this policy could serve you well.

Friday 27th

Listen to your intuition and don't ignore your instincts. Things that happen out of the blue during eclipse season can often show you where change is required. An argument or conflict could trigger what happens next. There is a volatile planetary energy today, so proceed cautiously.

Saturday 28th

Today's eclipse can help you to reassess your life and look at what works for you. Consider your energy levels, your health and the things you do every day. Wherever you're flagging or feeling stressed, this eclipse will point the way to a solution.

Sunday 29th

The more you understand yourself, the more you'll know what's required in life. If you're constantly feeling stressed or irritated, this may be a warning, so look at what you might need to attend to. Work and health are the key areas under the cosmic spotlight today.

Monday 30th

You may be juggling your schedule this week, especially if you're trying to keep other people happy. Do what you can but don't go too far, as this is not the time to stress yourself out. Learn to relax, perhaps through meditation, as doing so will benefit you in more ways than one.

Tuesday 31st

You might be back in the driving seat today and feel ready to get on with things. If a family member steps in to offer their help, you should consider accepting it. The more support you have in your life, the better. Your partner may want your advice on a personal issue.

NOVEMBER
· · · · · · · · · · · · · · · · · · ·

Wednesday 1st

Your perception of your life may now be distorted or out of
focus. Things could change quickly: one minute you might
think you have it all together, the next minute you're starting
to question reality. Go with the flow today, but don't make any
final decisions until this evening. Deal with facts, not fantasy.

Thursday 2nd

Some days it's easier to get to grips with the things in life that
you can deal with directly, and this could be one of those days.
It's in your close relationships where life could prove to be
perplexing right now, perhaps because there's someone in your
family who you can't get a handle on.

Friday 3rd

It's important to deal with facts, so don't let your imagination
run away with you now. It's easy to give yourself a hard time
and judge yourself poorly, but sometimes life is tricky to
negotiate, especially when you don't understand everyone
else's motives. Start by being kind to yourself.

Saturday 4th

If you're working overtime or constantly chasing deadlines,
you might feel out of sync. Try to find a more measured and
leisurely pace. If life has become all work and no play, it might
be time to make some changes. Any issues that emerge today
could point the way forward. Stay calm when possible.

. . . .

Sunday 5th

You might be pulled in different directions today; for example, you may have made a commitment to improve your health but find that you are offered junk food, or you might have a busy schedule but know that you need time to get ready for the week ahead. Be firm and do what's right for you.

Monday 6th

There may be a clash between your work life and your social life today. If something's got to give, decide where your priorities lie. Your partner may have one answer for you, but this could be in direct opposition to what you think is important. Feel your way forward carefully.

Tuesday 7th

Turn your brain to good use today by coming up with some imaginative ideas to make your life easier. The more relaxed and well-rested you are, the better prepared you will be to deal with what could be an exceptionally busy period. Put yourself and your needs first.

Wednesday 8th

There may be a shift in emphasis today. This is a potentially gentle period in the week which should serve as a reminder that relationships are important to your happiness. Even when your life gets busy, make time for the ones you love.

Thursday 9th

When you have the right people on your side, you can deal with anything in your life. Bear this in mind now and over the next few weeks. People power may be the missing ingredient you're looking for. It's a wonderful day for love and romance, so make the most of it.

Friday 10th

Your planet Mercury moves into your relationship zone today, so this will be a key time for partnerships in your life. You might be keen to prioritise your love life or consider a joint venture. Either way, be around people who lift you up and walk away from the person who puts you down.

Saturday 11th

Today might be especially emotional, and tempers may flare. Weigh up what's important in your life and prioritise your health. Try not to act on impulse, and wait instead for Monday's new moon to kick in.

Sunday 12th

There's more of an emphasis on water sign Scorpio now, and as an air sign, you could feel a little water-logged while emotions rule over logic. Try not to lose yourself in the intense murky waters of Scorpio. Don't sweat the small stuff and keep the bigger picture in mind.

Monday 13th

Today's new moon symbolises fresh beginnings. This may coincide with a busy period for you, especially while Scorpio rules your work and routine. It's a good time to look after yourself, so take care of your mind, body and soul. Events could turn quickly, so be ready.

Tuesday 14th

If a work situation has become untenable, do what you can to distance yourself. You may not be able to make an immediate change, but you can try to spend less time around a challenging person. Love could be the perfect antidote to any work or health stresses.

Wednesday 15th

If there's someone in your life you love spending time with, try to see them as often as possible, especially if this is a family member or new partner. The connections you make and the people you are instinctively drawn towards are where happiness can be found.

Thursday 16th

Consider putting some firm boundaries in place at work, especially if you have a tight deadline to meet. Close the door on other people and concentrate on the job at hand. The better your time management, the smoother your progress will be. Do whatever it takes to streamline your attention.

Friday 17th

A new routine could prove life changing, so look out for an opportunity to improve your health. Focus on your happiness and ensure that you're on the right track at work. Visualisation techniques could help you find your dream job.

Saturday 18th

You may need to decide where your priorities lie this weekend. If there has been an ongoing issue in your life, possibly linked to a financial situation or work role, consider giving yourself a break. If something is causing you too much stress, it might be better to knock it on the head.

Sunday 19th

Spend the morning with someone you love, such as a close family member. You'll enjoy being around people who are cheerful and happy. If you haven't been able to take a holiday or have a trip away recently, this could be the best time to make plans for 2024.

Monday 20th

When you have responsibilities in your life, it's easy to believe that there's no chance for freedom; however, that's not necessarily true, so make sure you reassess your options carefully. Use your people skills to win over a colleague, and think about starting a joint venture together.

Tuesday 21st

You may feel as if your options are limited right now, but a bold move could release you from a situation that's kept you trapped for some time. Finding the right job and creating the right partnerships in your life can help unlock the door to freedom. Don't be afraid to ask for help.

Wednesday 22nd

Engage with both your personal and professional relationships today. Find the right person to support you or get good legal advice if necessary. An expert opinion could help you break free from an emotional tie or a draining situation. Close the door to the past and focus on your future.

Thursday 23rd

You might find yourself handing control of a situation to a third party today. Take time to consider your next career move, especially if you're stuck in a job that's not right for you. If you get the right people on your side, you will prosper.

Friday 24th

Action planet Mars leaves your work and lifestyle zone today, so there should be less pressure on your everyday routine. This might mean that work commitments begin to ease, or a period of unemployment may come to an end.

Saturday 25th

You may have to consider permanently closing the door on someone today. This is never an easy decision, but if you know that things have to change, then it's time to make some tough choices. If there's someone in your life that you're missing a lot, find a way to remember them that comforts you.

Sunday 26th

A spooky turn of events could help make sense of things today. As a Gemini, you may often look out into the world for answers, but right now you're being encouraged to turn inward and find the answer that was there all along. Trust in your instincts and follow your intuition.

Monday 27th

Today's full moon is in your star sign, so the events of this weekend could prove to be revealing. Listen out for important insights, especially if you're confused or disillusioned. Speaking up in a partnership may not be easy, but this could be what needs to happen now.

Tuesday 28th

If there's someone you love, today might be the day to let them know. The powerful full moon energy lights up your relationships, so it's an ideal time to show that you care. While emotions can sometimes be a mystery, you don't always have to have everything worked out in your head.

Wednesday 29th

If you're working towards a long-term goal, you're in tune with your stars. However, you may have to dig deep to stay on track, especially if you're taking on a new learning challenge. If you're saving money for a major life shift in 2024, keep doing what you're doing and resolve not to give up.

Thursday 30th

Inner work can benefit you in so many different ways. Take time to focus on yourself and try to do what's right for you. This will help you to value yourself completely and feel good about the person you are.

DECEMBER

· · · · · · · · · · · · · · · · · ·

Friday 1st

Your planet Mercury moves into your finance zone, so money matters are under the cosmic spotlight. If there's anything you want to sort out before the end of the year, this is the best time to do so.

Saturday 2nd

It's a good day to make a firm decision around money. Try to avoid a big splurge, especially with Christmas shopping to think about. If you've experienced a debt situation in the past, it's especially important to be careful about what you spend.

Sunday 3rd

If you disagree with someone close when it comes to money and finances, this could prove to be the tipping point for an on-off relationship. If you're dealing with an ex, it's probably best to stand firm and do what's right for you.

Monday 4th

Venus, the planet of relating, enters your work zone today. This spells good news for teamwork and could help you to get the best colleagues on your side. Pay attention to money and ensure you're paid what you're worth. It's a good time to get things confirmed for the future.

Tuesday 5th

Look out for people who can help you at work. Dig a little deeper to find out what's hidden, especially if you're working with someone new. A person in a position of power may provide the support you're looking for.

Wednesday 6th

If you lose sight of the meaning of life, you might find it hard to visualise your future. Try to draw inspiration from the great thinkers throughout history. Look beyond the mundane and the everyday. Happiness is about feeling good inside.

Thursday 7th

Turn your attention towards love and relationships today. Whether you're seeking passion or a loving connection, there are some seriously good vibes about. It's a great day to put other people first, so try to spend quality time with those you love. Make space for laughter and fun.

Friday 8th

If you require some good fortune, today could be your lucky day. Make the most of this opportunity by doing something bold. If you use your skills wisely, you could make some serious progress with a long-term goal.

Saturday 9th

It's an excellent day to make new friends, especially if someone you work with invites you to a social event. If you want to improve your network, reach out to other people. You may have to dig deep to make an impact on others, but it's worth going for it.

Sunday 10th

If you're taking an extended holiday from work over the festive break, you'll be feeling pleased with yourself. Perhaps you've persuaded a colleague to stand in for you or you've found another way to free yourself from your commitments. Keep emotions out of the equation and carve out some free time.

Monday 11th

Work those connections and keep on the right side of the people who count. It's not what you know but who you know that will open doors for you over the next few weeks. If you're a typical Gemini, you'll know exactly what to say now, so use your communication skills to your advantage.

Tuesday 12th

Today's new moon lights up your relationship zone. This energy is dynamic and fast-paced, so look out for other people who can help you achieve your personal and professional goals. Someone new may dash into your life this week and sweep you off your feet.

Wednesday 13th

Communication planet Mercury turns retrograde today, which means that things could prove tricky regarding money matters. If you're experiencing issues with finances, proceed cautiously over the next few weeks. It's best to avoid getting carried away right now.

Thursday 14th

Mercury's in retreat, so it's a good time to take a closer look at money matters. Consider ways you can save money, even though finances may seem daunting at this time of year; doing so could prove to be a smart decision for the future.

Friday 15th

Look out for an opportunity to knock a debt on the head during the first month of 2024. Make sure that your money hasn't been disappearing down a black hole and consider plugging any wasteful outgoings or expenses.

Saturday 16th

If you're off on your travels this weekend or visiting friends who live in a different town, you're in tune with your stars. A change can be as good as a rest, so be sociable and expand your horizons. There's the potential for passion this evening.

Sunday 17th

If you're worried about where you're heading in life, now might be the moment to go with the flow and surrender to life's guidance. As a Gemini, you may find this challenging, but it's worth trying a new approach. You may feel guilty if a last-minute change of plan impacts a close relationship, but try not to worry too much.

Monday 18th

If you feel that you have an abundance of energy, this is a good time to share it with other people. Alternatively, you may be thankful for some support that comes your way. If you work hard, a charity event you're involved with might raise a huge amount of money and awareness.

Tuesday 19th

The key to success is to follow your passion and do what you love, so trust your feelings and go with the flow. Not everyone will be on your side now, so it might not be best idea to allow yourself to be persuaded by someone else.

Wednesday 20th

Catch up with your friends today and tomorrow by joining in with a group activity. It's a good time for a big party, but remember that it's not always sensible to get carried away. Anything goes when it comes to love right now, but don't forget that actions have consequences.

Thursday 21st

You might receive a welcome surprise today. However, if something fails to turn up or is delayed, you may have to wait until early 2024. Pay close attention to what's happening financially and double-check everything.

Friday 22nd

You may be ready to take a step back from work and want to relax before the festive break. Before you do so, engage with any important money matters. Watch out for something magical that could occur this evening.

Saturday 23rd

Your planet Mercury retreats into your relationship zone today, which means that you might be ready to get back in touch with an ex or someone from your past. However, it may be better to wait until tomorrow or the day after before reaching out. You might find that they get in touch with you first.

Sunday 24th

Take centre stage today, either at home with your family or in a position of leadership. Don't feel bad if you've decided to work the Christmas shift, as it's likely to pay well and give your reputation a boost. Keep your eye on the prize at work.

Monday 25th

The moon is in Gemini throughout Christmas Day, which is wonderful news, especially if you focus on what's right for you. Be sociable if you want to, eat and drink what you prefer and join in with the family quiz.

Tuesday 26th

It might be best to keep your opinion to yourself today as tempers are likely to flare first thing. If someone speaks out of turn, it might turn into a silent Boxing Day night. A family visit could turn out to be a bit of a disaster, so think twice before setting off.

. . . .

Wednesday 27th

Emotions are heightened during the full moon, and this could lead to a positive flow of energy in or out. Someone may surprise you with a gift or offer that benefits you, or you might be the one to reach out to help someone else.

Thursday 28th

Try to keep close tabs on reality, especially if you've felt lost in a fantasy world recently. You may find it a challenge to get a read on someone else, and this could lead to a disappointment. If in doubt, try to protect your heart.

Friday 29th

Love planet Venus enters your relationship zone today, so you can be sure of your feelings and the feelings of someone close. Something that happens this evening could make all the difference, especially if it involves a person who let you down previously. Let love in and practise forgiveness.

Saturday 30th

Your plans may change suddenly, which might lead you to pursue love rather than the social scene. Whatever decision you make, do what's right for you, and don't let anyone push you into a situation that you don't want to be in. You may experience a return to your past this evening.

Sunday 31st

New Year's Eve is a great time to be with your family or to enjoy yourself at home. Do whatever brings you comfort and make a wish that your world will expand and grow in the way you want it to in 2024.

Gemini

....

PEOPLE WHO SHARE
YOUR SIGN

PEOPLE WHO
SHARE YOUR SIGN
· · · · · · · · · · · · · · · · · ·

The voices of Geminians are loud, clear and capable of moving mountains. Their influential and contagious words often have a global impact, whether it's a story by Arthur Conan Doyle or a song from Bob Dylan. Discover the Geminians who share your birthday and see if you can spot the similarities.

22nd May

Novak Djokovic (1987), Maggie Q (1979), Ginnifer Goodwin (1978), Naomi Campbell (1970), George Best (1946), Laurence Olivier (1907), Arthur Conan Doyle (1859)

23rd May

Ryan Coogler (1986), Richard Ayoade (1977), Manuela Schwesig (1974), George Osborne (1971), Melissa McBride (1965), Drew Carey (1958), Marvelous Marvin Hagler (1954), Joan Collins (1933), Rosemary Clooney (1928)

24th May

Joey Logano (1990), Dermot O'Leary (1973), Eric Cantona (1966), Kristin Scott Thomas (1960), Priscilla Presley (1945), Patti LaBelle (1944), Bob Dylan (1941), Queen Victoria of the United Kingdom (1819)

25th May

Brec Bassinger (1999), Aly Raisman (1994), Roman Reigns (1985), Rasheeda (1982), Joe King (1980), Cillian Murphy (1976), Mike Myers (1963), Paul Weller (1958), Ian McKellen (1939)

26th May

Juan Cuadrado (1988), Scott Disick (1983), Lauryn Hill (1975), Helena Bonham Carter (1966), Lenny Kravitz (1964), Jeremy Corbyn (1949), Stevie Nicks (1948), John Wayne (1907)

27th May

Lily-Rose Depp (1999), André 3000 (1975), Jamie Oliver (1975), Paul Bettany (1971), Joseph Fiennes (1970), Paul Gascoigne (1967), Heston Blumenthal (1966), Henry Kissinger (1923), Christopher Lee (1922)

28th May

Cameron Boyce (1999), John Stones (1994), Carey Mulligan (1985), Jake Johnson (1978), Kylie Minogue (1968), John Fogerty (1945), Gladys Knight (1944)

29th May

Maika Monroe (1993), Riley Keough (1989), Melanie B (1975), Laverne Cox (1972), Noel Gallagher (1967), Carol Kirkwood (1962), La Toya Jackson (1956), Rebbie Jackson (1950), John F. Kennedy, U.S. President (1917)

30th May

Sean Giambrone (1999), Jake Short (1997), Jennifer Ellison (1983), Steven Gerrard (1980), Remy Ma (1980), Idina Menzel (1971), Mark Sheppard (1964)

31st May

Normani (1996), Azealia Banks (1991), Reggie Yates (1983), Colin Farrell (1976), Archie Panjabi (1972), Brooke Shields (1965), Lea Thompson (1961), Clint Eastwood (1930), Walt Whitman (1819)

1st June

Tom Holland (1996), Amy Schumer (1981), Alanis Morissette (1974), Heidi Klum (1973), Ronnie Wood (1947), Morgan Freeman (1937), Marilyn Monroe (1926)

2nd June

Sergio Agüero (1988), Morena Baccarin (1979), Dominic Cooper (1978), Justin Long (1978), Zachary Quinto (1977), A.J. Styles (1977), Wentworth Miller (1972), Andy Cohen (1968), Jeanine Pirro (1951), Charlie Watts (1941)

3rd June

Mario Götze (1992), Imogen Poots (1989), Michelle Keegan (1987), Rafael Nadal (1986), Anderson Cooper (1967), James Purefoy (1964), Susannah Constantine (1962), Allen Ginsberg (1926), Tony Curtis (1925), M. Karunanidhi (1924), King George V of the United Kingdom (1865)

4th June

Mackenzie Ziegler (2004), Lucky Blue Smith (1998), Brandon Jenner (1981), Russell Brand (1975), Angelina Jolie (1975), Izabella Scorupco (1970)

5th June

Troye Sivan (1995), Amanda Crew (1986), Pete Wentz (1979), Nick Kroll (1978), Mark Wahlberg (1971), Ron Livingston (1967), Rick Riordan (1964), Kathleen Kennedy (1953), Ken Follett (1949)

6th June

Ryan Higa (1990), Natalie Morales-Rhodes (1972), Paul Giamatti (1967), Jason Isaacs (1963), Colin Quinn (1959), Björn Borg (1956), Sukarno, Indonesian President (1901), Thomas Mann (1875)

7th June

George Ezra (1993), Emily Ratajkowski (1991), Iggy Azalea (1990), Michael Cera (1988), Anna Kournikova (1981), Bill Hader (1978), Bear Grylls (1974), Prince (1958), Liam Neeson (1952), Tom Jones (1940)

8th June

Rosanna Pansino (1985), Javier Mascherano (1984), Kanye West (1977), Shilpa Shetty (1975), Julianna Margulies (1966), Tim Berners-Lee (1955), Bonnie Tyler (1951), Nancy Sinatra (1940), Joan Rivers (1933), Jerry Stiller (1927), Barbara Bush (1925)

9th June

Tanya Burr (1989), Mae Whitman (1988), Natalie Portman (1981), Matt Bellamy (1978), Miroslav Klose (1978), Johnny Depp (1963), Michael J. Fox (1961), Aaron Sorkin (1961)

10th June

Kate Upton (1992), Faith Evans (1973), Bill Burr (1968), Elizabeth Hurley (1965), Jeanne Tripplehorn (1963), Carlo Ancelotti (1959), Judy Garland (1922), Prince Philip, Duke of Edinburgh (1921)

11th June

Kodak Black (1997), Claire Holt (1988), Joshua Jackson (1978), Peter Dinklage (1969), Hugh Laurie (1959), Gene Wilder (1933), Jacques Cousteau (1910)

12th June

Philippe Coutinho (1992), Dave Franco (1985), Kendra Wilkinson (1985), Adriana Lima (1981), Lil Duval (1977), Anne Frank (1929), George H. W. Bush, U.S. President (1924)

13th June

Aaron Taylor-Johnson (1990), Kat Dennings (1986), Mary-Kate and Ashley Olsen (1986), DJ Snake (1986), Chris Evans (1981), Steve-O (1974), Tim Allen (1953), Stellan Skarsgård (1951), W. B. Yeats (1865)

14th June

Lucy Hale (1989), Torrance Coombs (1983), Alan Carr (1976), Steffi Graf (1969), Donald Trump, U.S. President (1946), Che Guevara (1928)

15th June

Mohamed Salah (1992), Neil Patrick Harris (1973), Leah
Remini (1970), Courteney Cox (1964), Helen Hunt (1963), Xi
Jinping, General Secretary of the Communist Party of China
(1953), Erik Erikson (1902)

16th June

John Newman (1990), Daniel Brühl (1978), Eddie Cibrian
(1973), John Cho (1972), Tupac Shakur (1971), Jürgen Klopp
(1967), Stan Laurel (1890), Geronimo (1829)

17th June

Kendrick Lamar (1987), Marie Avgeropoulos (1986), Venus
Williams (1980), Sven Nys (1976), Tory Burch (1966), Greg
Kinnear (1963), Barry Manilow (1943), M. C. Escher (1898),
Igor Stravinsky (1882)

18th June

Willa Holland (1991), Pierre-Emerick Aubameyang (1989),
Josh Dun (1988), Richard Madden (1986), Blake Shelton
(1976), Isabella Rossellini (1952), Paul McCartney (1942),
Delia Smith (1941), Barack Obama Sr. (1936)

19th June

KSI (1993), Macklemore (1983), Aidan Turner (1983), Zoe
Saldana (1978), Laura Ingraham (1963), Paula Abdul (1962),
Salman Rushdie (1947)

20th June

Christopher Mintz-Plasse (1989), Mike Birbiglia (1978),
Quinton Jackson (1978), Frank Lampard (1978), Roy Nelson
(1976), Mateusz Morawiecki, Polish Prime Minister (1968),
Nicole Kidman (1967), John Goodman (1952), Lionel Richie
(1949), Brian Wilson (1942)

21st June

Lana Del Rey (1985), Prince William, Duke of Cambridge
(1982), Brandon Flowers (1981), Juliette Lewis (1973), Joko
Widodo, Indonesian President (1961), Michel Platini (1955),
Benazir Bhutto, Pakistani Prime Minister (1953)